WITHDRAWN

W9-BYI-840

dedication

This book is dedicated to the many creative

geniuses who visit and subscribe to the

Tera's Wish Web site and newsletter.

You humble and inspire me with your

enthusiasm for life and generosity of spirit.

acknowledgments

I knew I was in for the ride of my life when, the day after our marriage ceremony, my husband woke me with the words, "Thank you for not divorcing me yet!" After seven years, you still make me laugh, rub my back when I am whiny, believe in my talent when I'm not so sure and drive me crazy leaving dishes in the sink! Ken Mugrage, you are the love of my life. Thank you for not divorcing ME yet!

This book would not be in your hands today without the support and encouragement of Sally Finnegan at North Light Books. Sally is one of the most creative, generous and funny people I have ever met. Thank you for believing in this project, giving me champagne when I was crabby and not making me eat any of that chili when I visited you in Cincinnati!

I am blessed with a wonderful and fun family. I was not always an easy person to understand, but I always knew that I was loved and accepted. I send my love and gratitude to my parents, Curt and Marie Gemmil; my sister and brother and their families—Tonya, Bob and Natasha Mills and Curtis, Dolores and Madison Gemmil; my Uncle Hal and Aunt Alice Henry and my "Aunt" Rita Potter. When I

married, I was welcomed into the second wonderful and fun family of Bill and Ellen Mugrage, Bill Mugrage, Jr. and Deanna, Nicholas and LaDena Parks.

They say it takes a village to raise a child; the same might also be said about creating a book. My grateful thanks goes to my editor Liz Schneiders, book guru Tricia Waddell, photography genius Christine Polomsky and the many other people who put their heart and soul into creating this book. It is truly an honor to be part of such a talented group of people.

I want to acknowledge and thank my Lord and Savior, Jesus Christ. Any speck of talent I possess, and everything good I have ever accomplished, must be credited to God. Because of His love and faithfulness, I am here to write this book.

table of contents

An Introduction to Your Creative Journey 7

an introduction
to your creative journey

*W*hile most arts and crafts books teach a specific technique or skill, this book is more like a map to help you find the treasure that already resides within you.

My purpose is to be your travel guide. I will help you tap into the already unlimited potential of your ability to create and help you over the rough spots in the terrain by addressing common fears and blocks to creativity. Along the way, you will have the opportunity to try a variety of creative projects to help you through some of the fears and build your creative confidence.

I wrote this book with two audiences in mind: the first audience is the people who do not feel creative but have always had the desire to break through. The second audience is the struggling creatives who have discovered their own creativity but find themselves blocked in moving forward to do their best creative work.

In the following chapters, I address some of the most common blocks to creativity. As you read this, you may find that one of these blocks is a problem for you or you may find a combination of the blocks bother you at one time or another. You may choose to do the project and work through the exercises even if the specific block hasn't been a problem for you because you are intrigued or inspired by the information. Do whatever works best for you. You can't do this wrong!

In each chapter, you will find exercises and ideas for taking the things you have learned and spreading your creative wings a bit. Learning by copying has a fine tradition in the arts. Eventually, you will gain enough confidence to try some things that are your own. These exercises are meant to help you get started. At the end of each chapter, you will find a resource listing for books and/or Web sites if you want to learn more about the art form presented.

how to be creative:
listening to yourself

S ince we are going to spend some time together working on creativity, I'd like to tell you about my own creative awakening. Just as in my own life, it is never too late for you to rediscover your own creative talents.

To start your journey off right, you will learn a little bit about the nature of creativity. Lots of misconceptions surround what people think it means to be artistic or creative. It is so much more than you think!

Next, I will introduce you to the many blocks to creativity that affect many of us from time to time. It is important that you recognize these blocks and realize that you have the power within you to overcome each and every one of them. Each chapter is designed to build your creative confidence in a variety of creative and practical ways: through encouragement, exercises and lots of fun and inspiring craft projects. The reward that comes when you reclaim your creativity is tremendous, so let's get started!

creativity and me

If you have picked up this book, you know me. Although we have probably never met in person, you would recognize me if you saw me in a crowd, if only in spirit. I was the teenager who had good grades but dyed her hair pink. I was the twenty-something who dreamed of being an actress but kept a day job in a law office. I was the thirty-something who ran a company while hoarding books on painting, crafts and creativity but rarely took time to do those things.

Inside of me, in a place I rarely spoke of, I believed I had a talent—something that set me apart. I may have left my pink hair behind, but I dreamed of dancing, painting, writing, eating fabu-lous meals with even more fabulous people and living an epic life. All the while, even though I tried to stifle it, little bits of my creativity kept seeping out into my life.

For years I secretly blamed the taming of my soul on the people in my life. I had quit trying to be an actress because it made my mom nervous when I spent time in Hollywood. I hadn't written the books I wanted to write because I was just too busy trying to pay my bills and live the life I thought everyone expected of me.

Of course, those were just excuses. I had made the choice to quit auditioning and working in the city. I had not made the time for my own creativity. I was "too tired" to draft an outline for a book, but

I always seemed to have time to shop or watch TV or read yet another novel. It was just so much easier to blame someone else.

As much as I wanted to write, paint and be creative, I dismissed my creativity as inadequate, boring and not worth anything because I couldn't make "real" money at it and no one had ever told me I had any talent!

My life changed in the summer of 1998 when one of my dearest friends was diagnosed with cancer. Her name was Debbie Kaput and she was a rare jewel. She was a few years older than I was, and she had done many of the things I wanted to do—she was a published artist, showed her work and had two terrific kids. In short, she had everything to live for.

The last time we talked, she told me how cancer had changed her perspective and made her understand how much of her life she had wasted on worrying about the wrong things. She told me not to assume that I had a tomorrow to live my dreams, and that I needed to get to work making the life I was meant to live. I did not want to listen to her. When Debbie lost her battle with cancer, all I could think about was what she had said.

After Debbie's death, I wrote a sort of personal manifesto about creativity and living authentically to help me figure out what I really wanted in life. That became a Web site called "Tera's Wish" (www.teras-wish.com). Through the Web site, I have "talked" to thousands of people about creativity, art and living. I was astonished to find out how many people had the same feelings of creative inadequacy I had experienced. This book has come out of what I have learned from four years of writing and talking about creativity with people from all walks of life and exploring my own creative path.

creativity and you

My story may resonate with you completely or in a much smaller way. This book is not written as a manual for people who want to give up their day jobs and become full-time artists. It is for all the people I have met along the way who told me they were not creative at all but secretly longed to find their voice. It is for everyone who has told me a story about their talented mother or sister or friend who did amazing things creatively while they claimed they did not have a shred of talent. It is for the person whom, until now, may not have been able to admit that they really did want to be creative but didn't know how.

This book is a personal letter from me to you. In it, I address the most common fears about creativity that I have experienced myself and have heard from readers of my Web site and newsletter and participants in my seminars. You are not alone if you have ever stood in front of a worktable and felt inadequate or afraid of criticism, or wondered why you even bother. Everyone experiences some of those doubts at one time or another. I wrote for you the book that I wish I'd had when I was starting out on my creative journey. It is my hope that whether you dabble a few hours a month by making your own greeting cards or become a full-time artist someday, you will have an easier path to follow than I did.

Even if you have always denied being creative, there is some small voice inside of you that has never stopped whispering the dreams of your youth. You may have squashed that voice so effectively that it is barely audible, but you know it is there. You may know what the voice says but rationally know that there is absolutely no way you could ever accomplish it, so you shut it up any time it dares to pipe up and remind you of its presence.

It is time to listen to that longing. If your childhood dream was to be a prima ballerina and you are currently sixty-five years old with flat feet, you may think your dream is dead. You are wrong. You see, that was the dream of a child, but as an adult you can transform it into a grown-up dream that can fill your soul with joy. No, you may not dance the lead at Kennedy Center (but hey, you might!), but you can still dance for yourself, and that alone is well worth your time.

You were born with everything you need to be creative in the way you are meant to be creative. You don't have to wait for a muse to give you inspiration; you don't have to wait until you know everything about your craft. You only need to get still and listen to yourself. Trust the voice inside of you that has never really stopped telling you that you need to do this.

what is creativity?

MYTHS ABOUT CREATIVITY

Very often when I'm asked what I do for a living and I reveal that I am an artist, the questioner replies with the following statement: "I can't even draw a straight line!" This frustrates me terribly. After all, what is creative about drawing a straight line? I mean, when did that become a requirement?

I believe this response comes from our experiences in school and with other people who were creative in our eyes. It is true that some people have a gift for drawing, just as some people have an innate gift for cooking, sewing, dancing, arranging furniture or being a lawyer. However, few people have a gift for drawing, cooking, sewing, dancing, arranging furniture AND being a lawyer. We have an unfortunate tendency to compare ourselves to others and find ourselves lacking without considering that while we may not be as creative as we'd like in one area, we certainly have creativity and skill in other areas. We also live in an age where learning just about anything is possible—if you really want to learn it.

> [QUOTE]
>
> *Notice the difference between what happens when a man says to himself, 'I have failed three times,' and what happens when he says, 'I'm a failure.'*
>
> —S.I. Hayakawa

When I give seminars on creativity, I do the following exercise. I ask people to raise their hands if they "can't draw." Usually about 90 percent of the people in the seminar raise their hands. I ask them to pull out a pen or pencil and put an oval on their piece of paper, then I ask them to put a square next to it and then we move on to a squiggly line. When that is done, I ask everyone who completed those three figures to raise their hands. Usually 100 percent of the hands in the room go up. I then tell them, "Congratulations! You can draw! You may not draw as well as you would like, but that is a very different thing from not being able to draw at all."

Becoming as creative as you would like to be—or creative in the ways you would like to be creative—should be your aim.

CREATIVITY DEFINED

Creativity is just a word, but it is one with a lot of emotional impact for people who do not feel they are creative. If that fits you, it may be important to start your journey by examining your personal definition of creativity. If you have a limiting belief about what creativity is, then you may block yourself from getting started on a creative journey.

"Notice the difference between what happens when a man says to himself, 'I have failed three times,' and what happens when he says, 'I'm a failure.'" —S.I. Hayakawa

Words have great impact for many of us. If you have told yourself for years that you "can't" draw, you probably haven't made any attempt to learn to draw better. If you have told yourself you don't draw as well as you would like, you are more likely to have picked up books on drawing because that statement gives you room to improve.

According to *The American Heritage Dictionary of the English Language (Fourth Edition)*, creativity is defined as:

C

cre·a·tive

ADJ.
1. Having the ability or power to create: (Human beings are creative animals).
2. Productive; creating.
3. Characterized by originality and expressiveness; imaginative: (creative writing).

N.
One who displays productive originality: (the creatives in the advertising department).

Let's look at the definition of creativity given above. The first and second adjectival definitions revolve around the production of something creative. *The American Heritage Dictionary of the English Language* defines create as "to cause to exist; bring into being." In other words, if you can create something (bring into being), you are creative. Make a sandwich? Creative.

The third definition covers the creative process as "characterized by originality and expressiveness; imaginative." This is the gooey, messy part because there is no objective standard for what is "original," "expressive" or "imaginative." As a result, it can be easy to dismiss our efforts as lacking.

The words "creative" and "creativity" are sometimes incorrectly used to describe the characteristics of creativity, rather than the process itself. For example, you might call someone creative but really mean they are eccentric or you might call someone creative who is an innovator or very imaginative. The word "creativity" is most often used in the context of art, but it is important to understand that there is a difference between being "artistic" and being "creative." A lawyer can be intensely creative (and the best lawyers are) and not artistic at all.

A NEW WAY OF THINKING

The product of what we consider "creative" and the process of how we get there are simply problems to be solved. What color will you paint the sky? Into what shape will you bend the metal wire? How will you put the ingredients together for dinner? How will you solve the dispute with your neighbor? The more innovative or original you are with your solution, the more "creative" you are considered to be.

You make choices every day and use your creativity in every aspect of your life. How creative, innovative or original you are really depends on how confident you are in the specific arena of the problem you are facing. If you are confident in your ability to paint, then you are more likely to be daring and try an unusual color combination or technique. Likewise, if you are confident in your work, you are more likely to be willing to try something innovative to solve a problem.

In other words, creative confidence, like any other confidence, comes from experience and knowledge. Indeed, like a muscle, the more we exercise it, the more creative (or more able to look outside the box for answers) we become.

blocks to creativity

TYPES OF CREATIVE BLOCKS

There are two types of blocks that can bring us to a screeching halt creatively.

The first type of block comes out of fear and is usually voiced in the form of our inner critic. Depending on our personal insecurities, we might tell ourselves things like, "I'm not an artist," or "I'll look stupid in front of my friends if I try this."

The second type of block is the excuses we give ourselves for not doing the work. These include comparing our fledgling creative forays to the work of people far more experienced, using procrastination techniques like "waiting for inspiration" (that never comes) and so on.

THE "INNER CRITIC"

Number one on the hit parade of blocks is fear. Fear and doubt are a slippery slope. Once you give in to fear, it becomes harder and harder to climb back up to the top.

Have you ever tried *not* to think about the theme song from a TV show? Nope, don't think about it. *Do not* think about that song. Well, of course, in order *not* to think about something, you have to keep what you are supposed to *not* think about in your head. Every time you remind yourself not to think about it, you must think about it!

Doubts are like that. If someone who you respect or who is in authority over you has told you, for example, that you are not very good at painting, that comment will come charging back into your head every time you have to paint. It is an unfortunate aspect of the way our brains work. Like Pavlov's dogs and ringing bells, doubts are conditioned responses.

Often our fears come to us in the voice of our "inner critic." For example, if you were told you are not very good at painting, that person's voice or specific phrase they used to criticize your work might become your "inner critic" any time you need or want to paint. For some of us, the inner critic is one or both of our parents; for others it may be a teacher, sibling or other person whose opinion we respected at a vulnerable time in our lives.

I believe the inner critic is a self-preservation device to keep us from the pain of rejection or criticism. We use it to justify our procrastination (or failure to start at all) and we are often supported in that by the people around us. We can blame our inner critic and not have to try. We can let it cripple us and everyone shakes their head in sympathy because they've felt the lash of their own inner critic's tongue.

In chapters two through six, I address some of the most common voices. They are:

- **I'M NOT AN ARTIST.** I don't know how to draw, what colors to choose or how to put a design together.

- **I'M NOT GOOD ENOUGH.** Anything I would create would be worthless or boring. I have nothing interesting to contribute. It is a waste of time. Anything I would do would have no value because it has been done before or has been done better than I could do it.

- **I'LL NEVER LEARN ALL THE TECHNIQUES OF A CRAFT THAT I NEED, SO I NEVER GET STARTED.** I'll have to wait until I learn a lot more before I'll be ready to begin something new.

- **I GET STARTED ON A PROJECT AND THEN I JUST GO BLANK.** I feel like the well is dry and no matter what I do, I can't figure out how to finish the project. I know it isn't right, but I don't know how to fix it.

- **I'M AFRAID OF WHAT PEOPLE WILL THINK IF I CLAIM TO BE CREATIVE OR AN ARTIST.** I'll appear stupid or foolish to my friends and family.

You may have experienced one or all of these thoughts at one time or another, or your own inner critic may be specific to an experience in your life. Whatever the fear or criticism, you can get through it and start working creatively.

Whatever goes on inside your head belongs to you and you control it. It may not feel like it sometimes, but it is within your control. Your inner critic is just a conditioned response to specific stimuli. You can learn to change that response.

Remember the TV theme song—the one that you just couldn't get out of your head? Eventually it did stop—when you finally stopped thinking about it and became distracted by something else. In that way, the inner critic is something like a two-year-old having a tantrum: distract it, move on to something else and you will forget about it.

If you are dealing with a criticism specific to a situation in your life, write down the words or phrase that you hear from your inner critic and who said them to you originally. For example, if the critic was a teacher, write about how old you were when you received the criticism and what the circumstances were in your life (family, school and so on). Finally, as an adult looking back on the situation, write about whether the person who said the remark was qualified to judge what you were doing.

For example, I grew up thinking I was very clumsy and unathletic because other children and teachers often teased me about it. (The yearbook for my seventh-grade class even included a comment about how I was prone to trip and fall!) As an adult, I look back on that situation with new eyes. I had gone to school a year early, and the differences between a four-year-old and a five-year-old, both physically and in terms of coordination, are quite dramatic. Of course, I seemed clumsy and awkward compared to the other children in my class who were all a year farther along in their development than I was. This continued until I physically "caught up" to their development.

Look at the situations in your life that resulted in fears or doubts for you. Looking at the situation as an adult, you may find that the criticisms leveled at you were unfair or unjustified. When I realized that the age difference accounted for my "clumsiness" as a child, I decided to let go of those old feelings of ineptitude. I signed up for a martial arts class and redefined my feelings about who I was physically.

In the end, your desire to create must overcome that inner voice of doubt. Momentum will help you past your fear. To build momentum, you have to get started. The craft projects in this book, with their step-by-step instructions, are an excellent way to get moving.

GETTING PAST EXCUSES

In chapters seven, eight and nine, I will guide you through some of the common excuses we use to avoid creative pursuits. These include waiting for inspiration, comparing your work to other artists and getting through the learning process. We tend to use these blocks as an excuse to keep us from getting started.

When I taught painting, one of my great frustrations was that many of my students compared their work to my own from the start. They would not give themselves permission to be beginners. If you don't start as a beginner, you can't get to the intermediate or advanced levels in any art—even if you are starting with an innate talent. All creative work takes practice—even the greatest creative minds in history created horrible work some of the time.

Taking time to find your creative voice is important for what it gives to you—the joy of creation—and that is enough.

CREATIVE CONFIDENCE

All creative processes require courage. It takes bravery to take that first step toward doing anything new, but creative processes tend to generate even more fear than other first steps because they are, in a way, a birthing process. (And we all want our "kids" to be successful!)

Gathering the courage to create is a simple process. It starts by understanding that very little creativity springs from a void. Surround yourself with the tools you need, including instructional books like this one, so that if you hit a block you will have a place to start again. See what inspires and encourages you, be it making collages, topiaries or anything in between, and stick with it.

Like any skill, creativity comes through practice. If you do anything enough, you learn what works and what doesn't, and eventually you don't even have to think about it to do it well.

rubber stamping
a great impression

Rubber stamping is an excellent craft with which to begin your creative journey. Rather than starting "from scratch," rubber stamps give you a head start with an inspiring library of ready-made images. Stamp a favorite saying and image onto a greeting card or handmade stationery and the pleasure is practically instantaneous, making this craft a tremendous confidence-builder.

CREATIVITY SESSION: *The "Arteest"*

[CREATIVE BLOCK]

I'm not an artist. I don't know how to draw, what colors to choose or how to put a design together.

CONFIDENCE: THE KEY TO CREATIVITY

If you decided you wanted to become a housekeeper, chances are you would not let the fact that you were not born with the ability to iron perfectly, to know exactly what product would remove what stain or to know the proper way to fold a fitted sheet stop you from that path. After all, there are books on the subject, you know people who know how to do these things and you watch Martha Stewart religiously. This is a doable goal.

Being artistic is just as doable but we have a prejudice that tells us that artists are "born" as artists and we can't learn the necessary skills if we weren't born with those gifts. It is true that some people develop the skills to draw or paint at an early age. We all went to school with a few people who could draw well from memory. Their skill seemed to spring from them like water from a fountain.

Some people do have a gift for drawing but, like any skill, it requires practice to develop that skill. When we look at the art created by the masters, we are seeing the finished product of what

may have been years of work. Historically, artists apprenticed and copied the work of the great artists that preceded them to learn the skills for which they were later praised. Unfortunately, we tend to assume that these artists were born painting or drawing perfectly and dismiss the years of labor they put into honing those skills.

Although you may not consider yourself an artist today, you can learn the skills necessary to become one if you are willing to put in the time to become proficient. Now you may be saying, "But that will take forever" or "I don't have that much time!" There is an old saying about this: Do you know how old you will be by the time you learn that skill? The same age you will be if you don't!

Confidence is one of the keys to consistent creativity. Unfortunately, confidence isn't something you can buy or learn; it comes as you build a foundation of experience. Confidence frees you from worry and brings energy and enthusiasm to your work. It is built by taking risks, staying focused and making the effort to learn. The more projects you try, the more you will learn and the greater your confidence will be.

You may not be the artist you want to be today, but there is a world of information out there that you can use to teach you what you need to know. Confidence comes with experience, practice and time.

rubber stamping: getting started

JUST WALKING DOWN THE RUBBER STAMP AISLE OF YOUR LOCAL CRAFT STORE IS INSPIRING. And making greeting cards is just one of many creative ways to use rubber stamps. You need little more than some decorative paper or cardstock, some ink pads and a few good rubber stamps. The projects in this book use two common types of ink: dye ink and pigment or embossing ink. Quick-drying dye ink works best for applying bold color to coated paper. Embossing ink (also known as pigment ink), stays wet until heat set.

You can give a glossy, dimensional look to your stamped image when you sprinkle pigment ink with embossing powder and heat set it with an embossing gun. The embossing or heat gun is similar to a hair dryer, but it puts out a great deal more heat and less air so that the powder is not blown all over your work space. Both of the card making projects in this chapter will give you a chance to experiment with this wonderful technique.

Other supplies you might find useful when making rubber stamped cards include decorative-edged scissors, stamp cleaner, a ruler, a glue stick or other paper adhesive and a bone folder to score and press your papers flat.

confidence builders

✱ MAKE A SUCCESS LIST

One way to build your confidence when facing new situations is to remind yourself how many times you have conquered difficult situations in the past. This need not be limited to creative successes; list any challenge you have overcome, for example, graduating from high school, getting your driver's license, getting a promotion at work or taking a class.

Think about how many times you have done what you were sure you could not do. Think about the many moments that you were sure you would not make it through, and yet miraculously you are here. Think about the parties you were too scared to go to and yet went anyway. Think about the job interviews, the breakups and the tough projects you survived. Jot down all of these success stories in a little notebook or pin them where you can see them every day. All of it belongs to you. All of it is your history, but it is more than that. It is your proof of how strong and powerful you really can be.

✱ MAKE YOUR OWN CREATIVE ARSENAL

Feeling stuck? Surround yourself with inspirational and informational materials to help you through slumps or to provide background information for the creative process. Create your own arsenal of tools by collecting reference books, photographs and other items that you can use to answer your questions or get inspiration. You might also join an online group about the art or craft form you are learning so that you can ask questions of people who are interested in the subject.

paris montage card

Create this dramatic card while learning stamping basics! The juxtaposition of the black, white and red make this an appealing and fun project.

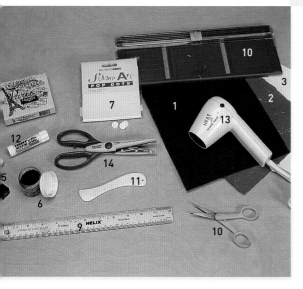

◀ MATERIALS

1 8½" x 11" (21.6 x 28cm) black handmade paper

2 8½" x 11" (21.6 x 28cm) red handmade paper with gold thread

3 8½" x 11" (21.6 x 28cm) white cardstock

4 rubber stamps (PSX: "New Lands" and "Paris Montage" stamps)

5 black embossing ink pad

6 black embossing powder

7 double-sided adhesive foam dots

8 black dye ink pad

9 cork-backed ruler

10 scissors or paper trimmer

11 bone folder

12 glue stick

13 embossing or heat gun

14 decorative scissors (Fiskars Colonial pattern)

1 ▪ Trim and Fold Your Paper

Trim the black paper to 10" x 7" (25.4 x 17.8cm) using a paper trimmer or scissors. Fold the paper in half to create a 5" x 7" (12.7 x 17.8cm) card.

tip When cutting paper, follow the old adage to measure twice and cut once!

2 ▪ Smooth the Folds

Use a bone folder to smooth the folded edge of the card. If you don't have a bone folder, you can use any smooth, hard item such as the side of a pen, a credit card or a CD case.

3 ▪ Tear the Red Paper

Trace a 6" x 4" (15.2 x 10.2cm) rectangle on the red paper with a pencil. Place a cork-backed ruler along each line and tear the excess paper away. This will create a soft, feathered edge that mimics the deckled edge of handmade paper.

tip You may find that slightly dampening the paper with a cotton swab along the line to be torn will make tearing easier.

4 ▪ Apply Glue to the Paper

With a glue stick, apply an even amount of glue to the entire back of the red paper. Pay close attention to the edges while applying the glue. If you tend to be messy, you can place scrap or wax paper under the piece so that you don't get glue on your work surface.

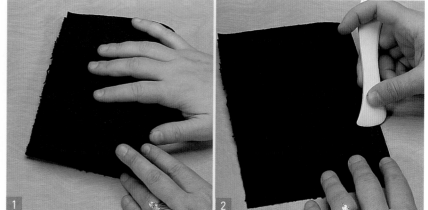

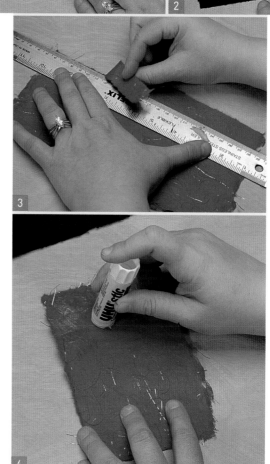

5 ▪ Glue the Paper to the Card
Apply the red paper to the center of the front of the card. Smooth the paper down with your hands or your bone folder, taking care to remove any air bubbles and to make sure the edges adhere to the surface.

6 ▪ Apply Embossing Ink to the Stamp
Apply black embossing ink to the Paris Montage stamp. If you hold the stamp in one hand and apply the ink with the other hand, you may have better control over the application of the ink.

7 ▪ Stamp the Image Onto Cardstock
Press your stamp onto a sheet of white cardstock. Use both hands to apply even downward pressure without rocking the stamp onto its edges.

8 ▪ Pour on the Embossing Powder
Apply a generous amount of black embossing powder directly over the stamped image. You will recycle the unused powder, so don't be afraid to put too much powder on the image. Gently shake the card to spread the powder evenly over the wet ink.

Choose the Right Ink • EMBOSSING INK is a thick, slow-drying ink that gives you time to apply and heat set embossing powder over an image. The ink will remain "open" (undried) for several hours, so you do not need to rush to apply embossing powder.

DYE INKS, on the other hand, dry much more quickly and cannot be used for embossing techniques. The bold, brilliant colors of dye inks are good for coloring in backgrounds and stamping text. Dye inks will sometimes bleed on uncoated paper, so try stamping your inks on a piece of scrap paper first.

9 ▪ Brush Off the Excess Powder

Over a clean sheet of scrap paper, tip the stamped sheet up on an angle and gently tap the sides. The powder should easily tap away from the areas without embossing ink. Use the scrap paper like a funnel to transfer any unused powder back to its container.

tip If you find that you cannot get the powder off the uninked portions of the card, wipe a used static-cling dryer sheet over the paper before stamping.

10 ▪ Heat the Image With an Embossing Gun

With a heat gun, heat the ink and powder. Continuously move the heat gun in small circles so as not to burn the paper. As the powder heats, you will see it melt together and form a satiny sheen. As each area hardens, move the gun to another area until the entire image is set.

11 ▪ Cut Out the Embossed Image

Trim around the embossed image, leaving about a ⅛" (.3cm) border. Peel five double-sided adhesive foam dots and apply them at the corners and center of the back of the embossed cardstock.

12 ▪ Attach the Image to the Card

Affix the cardstock in place on an angle over the red paper. Press down lightly to secure.

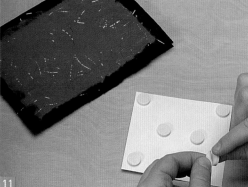

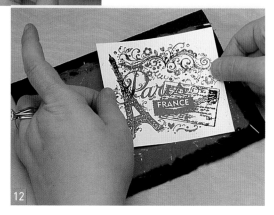

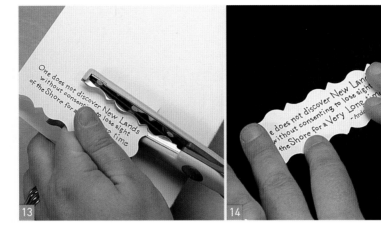

13 ▪ **Stamp the Quote With Dye Ink**

With black dye ink, stamp the "New Lands" quote on white cardstock, and then trim around it with decorative scissors.

14 ▪ **Glue the Quote Onto the Card**

Apply glue with a glue stick to the back of the white cardstock and apply it to the inside of the black card. Press down firmly with both hands to secure the image to the paper.

Clean Your Stamps ▪

Clean your stamps between uses, especially if you've used embossing ink, as this ink will not dry on the rubber. Many specialty stamp cleaners provide a scrubber top to work the cleanser into the nooks and crannies of the stamp. Simply apply the cleaning solution and then wipe the stamp with a paper towel or soft cloth to remove the ink.

If you don't have a commercial cleaner, try cleaning your stamps on a painting pad (the type used to paint walls) dampened with window cleaner. When you're finished, store your stamps out of direct sunlight.

✳ create an idea nursery

Another excellent resource for inspiration is what I call an Idea Nursery. You can create one by gathering magazine clippings, quotes, color swatches and images into a large sketchbook. Clip and save anything you are drawn to.

Later, look for common themes, such as color or design, when you pull all the clippings together to paste them into your book. When you are in need of inspiration, use the book to brainstorm ideas. For example, the colors from an ad might inspire you, or you may make something that you think would look good in a room featured in a photo.

RUBBER STAMPING (**PROJECT TWO**)

deco
geisha card

Once you have experience with the basics of
stamping and embossing, you can try your hand
at adding textures and decorative elements, such
as tassels and charms. The Deco Geisha card
uses the skills you learned in creating the Paris
Montage card, and takes it a step further by
adding a bit of embellishment!

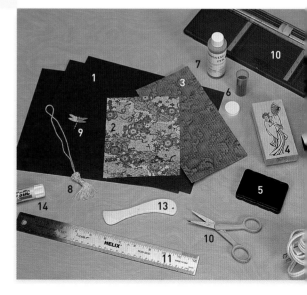

MATERIALS →

1 8½" x 11" (21.6 x 28cm)
forest green cardstock

2 9" x 12" (23 x 30.5cm)
Crepe Yuzen paper
(Hero Arts)

3 4½" x 4½" (11.4 x
11.4cm) piece of
corrugated cardboard

4 rubber stamp
(JudiKins: "Deco Geisha"
stamp)

5 black embossing ink
pad

6 antique gold
embossing powder

7 clear embossing ink

8 cream decorative
tassel

9 dragonfly charm

10 scissors or paper
trimmer

11 cork-backed ruler

12 embossing or heat
gun

13 bone folder

14 glue stick

1 ▪ Trim Your Paper

Using a paper trimmer or scissors, cut
out two pieces of green cardstock. Cut
the first piece to 10" x 7" (25.4 x 17.8cm)
and fold it in half to form the base of your
card. Cut the second piece of green cardstock to 2" x 4⅛" (5.1 x 10.5cm). Cut the
decorative Crepe Yuzen paper to 3½" x 5½"
(8.9 x 14cm), and cut the corrugated cardboard to 2½" x 4½" (6.4 x 11.4cm).

2 ▪ Ink the Stamp

Apply black embossing ink to the Deco
Geisha stamp by patting the entire surface of the stamp with the ink pad.

3 ▪ Stamp the Image and Add the Embossing Powder

Press the inked stamp firmly onto the
smaller 2" x 4⅛" (5.1 x 10.5cm) piece of
green cardstock. Pour a generous
amount of gold embossing powder over
the stamped surface.

Tip the paper up on an angle and gently
tap the excess powder onto a clean sheet
of paper. Use this sheet like a funnel to
transfer unused powder back into its
container. Brush away excess powder
with a small, clean brush, but be careful
not to smear your image.

4 ▪ Heat the Image With an Embossing Gun

With an embossing gun, gently heat the
ink and powder. Continuously move the
heat gun in small circles so as not to
burn the paper. As the gold embossing
powder heats, you will see it change color
and become very metallic as it sets.

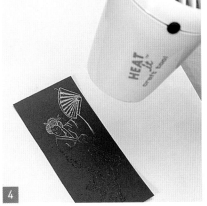

Make a Good Impression

THERE ARE MANY WAYS to apply ink to your stamp. Use the one that feels most comfortable to you. You may prefer to hold larger stamps in your hand. For smaller stamps, the traditional "press down" method often works best. Whatever works for you is right!

When you stamp your image, apply your hand firmly on the back of the stamp but do not rock the stamp or you may get a shadow line on your paper. With just a little bit of practice, you'll leave a great impression every time.

5 ▪ Fold the Card and Glue on the Papers

Fold the 10" x 7" (25.4 x 17.8cm) cardstock in half to create a 5" x 7" (12.7 x 17.8cm) card. Smooth the folded edge with a bone folder. With a glue stick, glue each piece of paper in place onto the front of the card as shown in the photo to the right.

tip If you want your card to be saved as a keepsake, use acid-free paper and a glue stick.

6 ▪ Smooth Down the Edges With a Bone Folder

Use a bone folder to make sure that each piece of paper is well adhered to the piece below it. Be especially careful that the embossed geisha image is completely glued to the ridges of the corrugated cardboard.

7 ▪ Add a Pool of Embossing Ink

To embed the tassel and charm, begin by applying a generous dab of clear embossing ink to the left corner of the card over the decorative Crepe Yuzen paper.

8 ▪ Pour on the Gold Embossing Powder

Sprinkle a generous amount of gold embossing powder over the clear embossing ink to give it some color.

9 ▪ Add the Tassel

Cut the loop of the tassel off ½" (1.3cm) above the knot. Carefully embed the tip of the tassel into the pool of embossing ink. Pour a small amount of extra embossing powder over the top of the tassel.

tip You may want to heat the embossing powder again before applying the tassel to hold it in place.

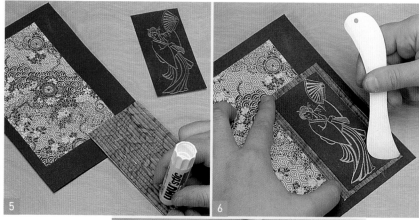

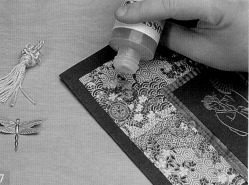

10 ▪ Heat the Powder to Set the Tassel
With an embossing gun, gently heat the ink and the powder to set the tassel in place. Continuously move the heat gun in small circles.

11 ▪ Press the Charm Into Place
While the embossing powder is still warm, push the dragonfly charm down into the puddle. When it dries, the melted embossing powder will hold the charm into place.

More Ways to Explore Rubber Stamping

- STAMP WITH DYE INK on torn bits of colored tissue paper, then use these scraps to découpage lamp shades, glass candleholders and suncatchers.

- MAKE CUSTOM GIFT BAGS by stamping over inexpensive colored bags.

- MAKE YOUR OWN RUBBER STAMPS by drawing a design on a rubber eraser. Carve out the negative space with a narrow-blade craft knife or linoleum cutter.

- PURCHASE SPECIAL HEAT-SET INKS for fabric so you can use the techniques you have learned on home décor surfaces such as pillowcases, lamp shades, shirts and purses.

- COLOR IN LARGE STAMPED IMAGES of flowers with chalks, watercolors or colored pencils.

✳ finding your stamping muses

✳ *Mary Jo McGraw is a well-known rubber stamp instructor and author. If you wish to make more greeting cards, look for her rubber stamp technique books at your local craft store or visit her Web site at www.maryjomcgraw.com.*

✳ *Subscribe to one of the many rubber stamp craft magazines available wherever crafts are sold. The Rubber Stamper, Somerset Studio and RubberStampMadness each has its own personality. Find inspiration in the one that appeals to your style.*

✳ *Visit a store that specializes in rubber stamping supplies. If they offer classes, consider taking one. If there is no rubber stamp store near you there are several resources online, including Gingerwood (www.gingerstamp.com) and Addicted to Rubber Stamps (www.addictedtorubberstamps.com).*

decorative painting
a stroke of brilliance

*P*ainting is much easier than you think. The beauty of the craft of decorative painting is that it is taught through detailed, step-by-step instructions that anyone can learn. And once you practice a few basic strokes, you can decorate any surface that appeals to you. So let go, take it a stroke at a time and enjoy!

CREATIVITY SESSION: *Trust, Value, and Worthiness*

[CREATIVE BLOCK]

I'm not good enough. Anything I would create would be worthless or boring. I have nothing interesting to contribute. It is a waste of time. Anything I do would have no value because it has been done before or has been done better than I could do it.

TRUST IN THE PROCESS

Even though I have been a professional artist for several years, occasionally I will start a design and simply panic. I hear that voice in my head that says, "Maybe I don't have any talent. Maybe I really can't design. Maybe I've just been kidding myself!"

Then I remember about trust.

Something I have come to believe about creativity is that you have to trust in the process. You have to trust that no matter how many times you have to start over, somewhere inside of you is the answer. As long as you live, you have unlimited chances to get it right. With each attempt, you learn. You learn that you can make mistakes and get past them. You discard what doesn't work and replace it with what does. You don't lose anything. You gain experience, you gain practice and that is the journey.

The worst thing that can happen is for you to give up. Creating is part of our essence. If we lose our faith in our ability to create—not to get it perfect the first time, but to keep trying and learning—we will stagnate.

We live in an instant society where we expect results like an order at a fast-food restaurant. Creativity isn't like that. Sometimes it takes days, sometimes years. You have to keep moving and trying, and trust in that smaller voice that got you started in the first place—the one that says, "I can do this. I have something to share."

YOU ARE WORTH IT

We live in a time where things that are valued tend to be those that have a monetary value. The problem with this type of thinking is it assumes that it is not enough to do something just because it makes you happy or brings you joy.

After the death of her mother, artist Lorraine Ulen wrote:

"My mother crocheted beautifully, but like many women, felt she needed to put everyone and everything else before her own desire to create. When she died, she left a clean house, a closet full of things saved for 'good' and a smattering of items she had made. I wish she had left a lot more dust and many more things I could hold and know her hands had made them. I wish she had felt herself worthy of the good china and linens, and the joy that she felt when she finished a delicate piece of clothing. I know that I felt she was worthy of them."

You must acknowledge that you are worthy of the time you need for your creative work—and your creativity is worthy of the time you give it. You can create miracles and masterpieces if you decide you want to, but you must devote time to developing your own creative voice.

decorative painting:
getting started

TO TRY YOUR HAND AT DECORATIVE PAINTING, ALL YOU NEED ARE A FEW PAINTS, A BRUSH OR TWO AND A SURFACE ON WHICH TO PAINT.

If you are working on wood, acrylic paint works very well and comes in a wide range of premixed colors. You will also need a sealer and varnish. Sealer is applied before you paint. It provides a clean, even surface and protects the paint from any dirt or irregularities in the wood. Varnish is used when the painting is complete to protect the painted surface.

Painting on glass is even simpler. All you really need is glass paint, which is sold at most craft stores. You don't need sealer or varnish; simply clean the glass thoroughly with isopropyl alcohol or a surface cleaner recommended by the glass paint manufacturer before you begin. Some glass paints also need to be heat set in an oven after they are applied. Read the instructions on the bottle to assure you get the best results.

Buy the best brushes you can afford. I like an acrylic/sable blend because the brush is absorbent but also has good "spring" to it—meaning it isn't floppy and is easier to control. Take good care of your brushes and they will last a long time. Do not leave them soaking in water for long periods of time or allow paint to dry on the bristles.

You will also need a water basin and palette. I use a wax palette, but a plate, piece of wax paper or tinfoil will also work when you are just getting started.

confidence builders

✳ TAKE IT STEP BY STEP

If you are feeling insecure, try projects that give you the safety net of step-by-step instructions. These might include painting, needle-work, woodworking or mosaics. Some people feel more confident going to classes or workshops to learn. If that makes you uncomfortable, remember there are many books and videos that can show you how to recreate a project at home or wherever you feel comfortable creating.

✳ WORK AT YOUR LEVEL

Give yourself a break! You are not going to like the outcome of every project you attempt. Sometimes it's because you attempt something more ambitious than you are ready for, but sometimes the instructions may not be written as well as they could be!

Before buying a book, be sure to look at the supply lists and instructions. Just because a project looks easy doesn't mean that the instructions are written for someone at your skill level. Make it easy on yourself by looking over instructions to make sure you feel comfortable with them before attempting the project.

basic brush techniques

The magic of decorative painting comes from combining a few basic brushstrokes in dozens of surprisingly beautiful ways. By learning to carefully load your brush and hold it properly when you paint, you can quickly create leaves, vines and colorful flowers to decorate any surface. If you have never painted before, practice the techniques on the following few pages until you gain the confidence you need to work on the whimsical box that follows.

Wax paper or children's finger-painting paper makes a reusable practice surface. Because of the waxy coating, acrylic paint will wipe off, so you can use your practice surface again and again.

THE DOUBLE-LOADED BRUSH

"Double loading" is a method for loading a brush with two different colors of paint so that the colors are carefully blended in the center of the brush. Follow these brush-loading techniques to create beautiful, softly shaded leaves and petals.

1 ▪ Dip One End Into the First Color
Start by putting two small puddles of fresh paint in two different colors on your palette. Wet a no.14 flat brush with water and blot it on a paper towel, leaving the bristles damp but not wet. Hold the brush on a slight angle and lift a dab of paint from the side of the puddle onto the corner of the brush.

2 ▪ Dip the Second End in the Other Color Flip the brush over so that the clean side is toward the paint puddle, and lift a dab of the second color onto the brush. You should have about the same amount of paint on both corners of the brush. Remember to lift the paint from the edge of the puddle so that you can control the amount of paint in the brush.

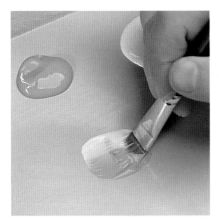

3 ▪ Start to Blend the Paint on the Brush
Holding your brush handle perpendicular to your palette and bracing your hand as you would when writing, blend the two colors together on the brush by stroking the brush all the way down to the "flat" or side of the bristles.

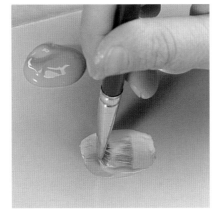

4 ▪ Finish Blending the Paint Stroke your brush in the opposite direction so that you blend the paint on the opposite side of the brush as well. Alternate the direction of your strokes until the paint is fully blended on both sides. Brace your hand so that you do not drift left or right, and stroke your brush in the same spot on your palette so that you don't have to reload the brush too often.

The brush is blended properly when color in the center is a mix of the two colors but the original colors remain at each end. You may have to go back and add paint to your brush until you have achieved an even blend. There is no need to clean your brush until you are finished painting unless the colors start to look muddy.

PAINTING FINE, WAVY LINES

Wavy lines are good for adding a bit of whimsy to any project. This technique is also good for making vines to dress up with leaves and flowers.

1 ▪ Thin Your Paint With Water Place a puddle of acrylic paint on your palette and thin it with water from a no. 2 liner brush until the paint is the consistency of ink and flows easily from your brush. Load the brush completely by stroking it through the thinned paint several times.

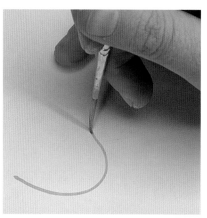

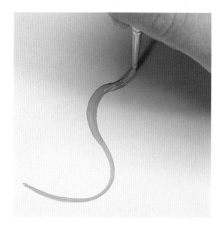

2 ▪ Make Fine Lines With Your Brush Tip To create a fine line, use only the very tip of the brush. Brace your hand with your pinkie finger or the side of your hand much as you would when holding a pen. It is important to hold the brush handle perpendicular to your surface so that you are using the tip and not the side of the bristles.

3 ▪ Press Down for Thicker Lines To get a wider line, apply more downward pressure on the liner brush. Once again, keep the brush handle perpendicular to your surface and brace your hand to control the brush more easily. Varying the thickness of your lines will add character and originality to your painting.

PAINTING LEAVES

Load a no. 12 flat brush following the double-loading technique on the previous page, then follow the steps to the right. This leaf is called a "one-stroke leaf" because you create it with a single stroke of the brush. The two colors on the brush create a shaded effect that gives the leaf depth.

1 ▪ Splay the Brush Out Flat With your hand braced, push the brush down to the flat so that the sides of the bristles are on your surface. The splay of the bristles will create the rounded edge of the leaf.

2 ▪ Turn the Brush to Form the Tip of the Leaf Pull your brush in the direction you want your leaf as you lift the downward pressure and turn the brush one-quarter turn. End the stroke with the

bristles at the chisel edge (over the very tips of the bristles). The turning of the brush as you lift creates the pointed tip of your leaf.

tip For smaller leaves, you can substitute a no. 6 filbert brush.

PAINTING ROSEBUDS

Once you have practiced the leaves and wavy lines, the rosebuds are a snap! With a clean brush, double load a no. 14 flat brush with white and rose acrylic paint.

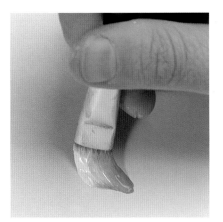

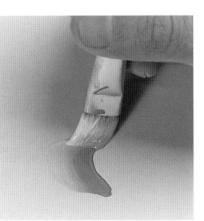

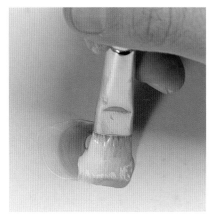

1 ▪ Begin the First Stroke Double load your brush with rose and white paint. Picture the top of the rosebud as an upside-down "U" shape with the white side of your brush at the top. Start with your brush on the chisel edge and pull it upward and to the right. When you get to the curve, apply downward pressure to widen the stroke.

2 ▪ Curve Down to Finish the Top Begin to ease the downward pressure on the brush as you curve back down the other side of the "U" until the brush is back up on the chisel edge.

tip The most common mistake is not starting and ending the stroke with the brush at the chisel edge. As you paint, think "chisel-flat-chisel."

3 ▪ Begin the Second Stroke Reload your brush with more paint and blend it well on your palette. Again, begin with your brush on the chisel edge and and the white paint at the top. Start from the same spot as before, but this time form a rightside-up "U." Pull the brush down, adding pressure at the bottom of the "U."

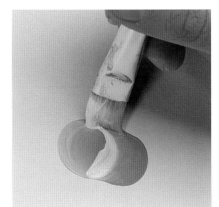

5 ▪ Paint the Calyx Load your liner brush with thinned green paint. Finish your rosebud by painting a few fine, wavy lines from the base of the rosebud to form the calyx.

4 ▪ Finish the "U" Stroke Complete the stroke by lifting the pressure and curving the stroke upward to finish the "U." The stroke should end with the the brush back up on its chisel edge. The second stroke should overlap the first so that you cannot see the background in between.

DECORATIVE PAINTING (**PROJECT ONE**)

whimsical painted box

This charming box with its ball feet and top knob makes a delightful conversation piece for your home. You can use it to hold some of the new art supplies you are collecting as well!

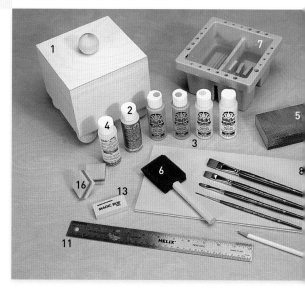

MATERIALS

1 6¼" x 6¼" x 7½" (15.9 x 15.9 x 19cm) ballfoot box

2 matte sealer

3 yellow, pink, yellow green and white acrylic paints (Folk Art Sunflower, Rose Pink, Fresh Foliage and Wicker White)

4 satin varnish

5 sanding block

6 foam craft brush

7 water basin

8 wax palette or plate

9 no. 20 flat brush

10 pencil

11 cork-backed ruler

12 no. 14 flat brush

13 eraser

14 no. 2 liner brush

[optional]

15 no.6 filbert brush

16 sponges

1 ▪ Seal the Wood Surface

Lightly sand the surface of the box, then apply wood sealer with a foam craft brush or flat brush. Be sure to saturate the wood well for maximum protection. Set the box aside to dry completely.

2 ▪ Sand the Box

After the sealer has dried, lightly sand the box again to smooth the grain down. This will make your paint go on smoothly and evenly.

3 ▪ Paint the Sides and Top Yellow

With a no. 20 flat brush, paint the sides and top of the box with Sunflower. It may take more than one coat to get complete coverage.

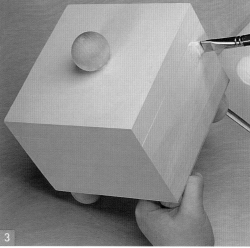

Preparing Your Surface •

WITH THE TECHNIQUES YOU LEARN in this chapter, you can paint on virtually any surface. The key to painting is to use the correct sealer and paint for the surface you choose. Craft and home décor manufacturers make paint and sealer for glass, plastic, wood, walls, metal and more! Preparing your surface properly will ensure that your painting will not peel or fade over time.

4 ▪ Paint the Bottom and Feet Pink

With the same brush, paint the bottom of the box and the ball feet with Rose Pink. By painting the entire bottom of the box a single color, you save time because you don't have to tape off and paint the ball feet separately.

5 ▪ Mark Off the Squares on the Box Sides

With a pencil and a ruler, lightly mark off 1½" (3.8cm) squares around the sides of the box in a checkerboard pattern. I prefer to use a cork-backed ruler because the cork prevents the ruler from sliding as you draw your lines.

6 ▪ Paint a Checkerboard on the Sides

Paint every other square around all sides of the box with Fresh Foliage using the no. 20 flat brush.

tip It is better to apply two thinner coats of paint rather than one thick coat that will not dry evenly. Thicker coats of paint are also more likely to drip and show brush lines.

7 ▪ Paint Vines Around the Box Lid

On your palette paper, practice using the liner brush before working on the box. Now paint a curvy line around the box lid. Vary the downward pressure on the brush so that the lines vary in thickness as they would in vines. Once the main wreath line is painted, paint six to ten wavy vines coming off the main vine until you have a simple wreath.

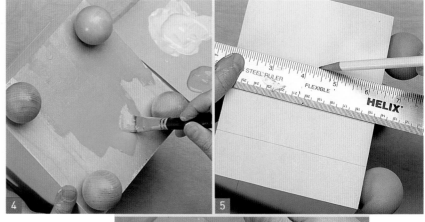

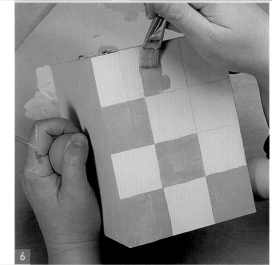

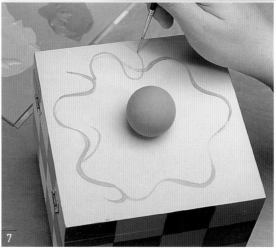

8 ▪ Add Leaves to the Wreath

Practice painting leaves on your palette or a piece of paper until you are ready to paint on your box. Paint leaves in a random pattern around the wreath with a no. 14 flat brush. Move the box so that your arm is never at an awkward position. Be sure to paint leaves going in more than one direction.

9 ▪ Add Rosebuds to the Design

Paint rosebuds in a random pattern around the lid with a no. 14 flat brush. There are nine roses painted on the box shown here. Paint the roses over and around the vines. The buds can also overlap the leaves.

10 ▪ Finish the Rosebuds

Load your liner brush with Fresh Foliage thinned with water, just as you did for the wreath lines. Paint the calyxes around the buds.

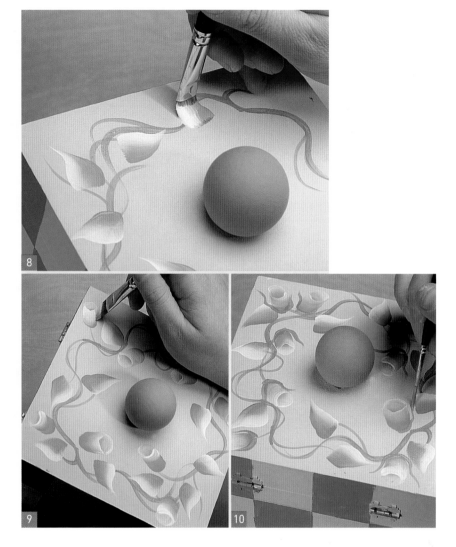

The Importance of Good Brushes • AN EXPERI-

ENCED PAINTER can get a good result with a bad brush because they know how to control a brush and how to compensate for problems.

Unfortunately, many beginning painters buy inexpensive brushes and then become discouraged with the results. Buy the best brushes you can afford. I suggest a good blend of synthetic and quality sable filaments, such as the Robert Simmons Sapphire brush line I use in this book.

11 ▪ Connect the Roses to the Vines
With your liner brush and the thinned
Fresh Foliage, paint vines to each of the
rosebuds and leaves. You may also want
to add a few additional squiggly vine lines
to even out the design.

**12 ▪ Dip the Brush Handle Into the
Yellow Paint**
Using the handle of your liner brush, dip
into a fresh pool of Sunflower.

**13 ▪ Paint Dots on the Feet and Knob
on the Lid**
Place a random pattern of dots on the ball
feet and knob on the lid of the box. Don't
worry about making each dot the same
size. A bit of variety looks good because
of the whimsical nature of this design.

**14 ▪ Paint Wavy Lines Along the
Checkerboard**
Load your liner brush with Wicker White
thinned with water and paint wavy lines
along the horizontal and vertical edges of
the checkerboard on the sides of the box.

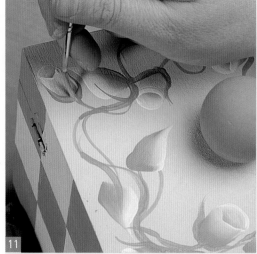

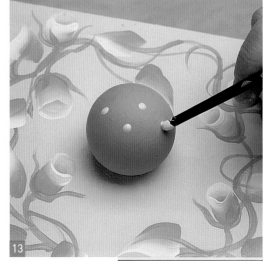

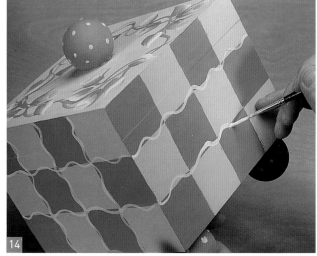

15 ▪ Varnish the Box

Allow the paint to dry for several hours. The dots on the knob and ball feet can take longer to dry, so check them before proceeding. Apply two coats of satin varnish. Allow the varnish to dry well before handling the box.

variation

[PAINTED JOURNAL COVER] Pretty leaves and roses can be painted onto just about any surface, including this blank journal cover.

✳ where to find further inspiration

Dozens of books and videos are available if you are looking for more projects to paint.

✳ **The Complete Book of Decorative Painting**
by Tera Leigh (North Light Books)

✳ **Priscilla Hauser's Book of Decorative Painting**
by Priscilla Wait Hauser (North Light Books)

✳ **Conversations in Paint**
by Charles Dunn (Workman Publishing Company)

✳ **Elegant Porcelain and Glass Painting Projects**
by Carin Heiden Atkins (North Light Books)

✳ choose your own colors

If the bright colors of this box do not appeal to you, spread your creative wings by choosing new colors. Each creative step you take will build your confidence and make the next step easier.

DECORATIVE PAINTING (**PROJECT TWO**)

fishbowl glass vase

A bit of paint can be just the thing to add some splash to your creative life. Grab a vase or glass bowl gathering dust in your cabinet and give it new life with the skills you learn in this project.

MATERIALS →

1 5" (12.7cm) glass vase with fluted edge

2 paper towel

3 isopropyl alcohol

4 white glass paint (Pébéo Vitrea 160 Veil White)

5 gold transparent outliner (Pébéo Vitrea 160 Gold)

6 no. 8 round brush

[not shown]

7 water basin

8 wax palette or plate

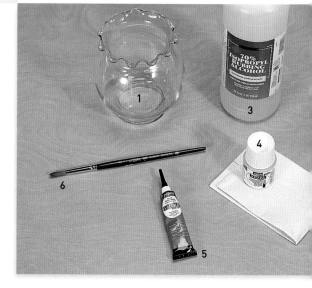

1 ▪ Clean the Glass

Before you begin painting, clean the glass
thoroughly with isopropyl alcohol to
remove any dirt and oil. Some glass
paints have their own surface conditioner
that is recommended, so be sure to read
the instructions on the paint before you
start. Handle the glass with care after it is
cleaned.

2 ▪ Begin the Petal Stroke

With the no. 8 round brush loaded in Veil
White, form the petals by painting a stroke
that goes from thick to thin at the center
of the flower. Begin by touching the tip of
the brush to the surface and applying
downward pressure toward the surface to
spread the bristles.

tip If you are concerned about making
mistakes, practice on a piece of paper
first, then on your glass vase.

3 ▪ Finish the Petal Stroke

Pull the brush in the direction of the stroke
by moving your arm, not just your hand.
Gradually decrease the pressure until only
the tip of the brush touches the surface.
This will be easiest if you can brace your
painting hand (using your pinkie finger) on
the glass or the table.

4 ▪ Paint Five Petals on Each Flower

Continue around the flower until you have
painted five petals roughly at two, five,
seven, ten and twelve o'clock. Do not
worry about making the strokes perfect or
even. Be sure to leave space at the center
of the petals for the flower center.

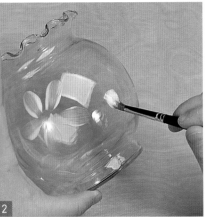

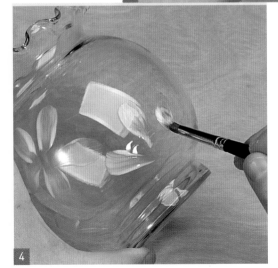

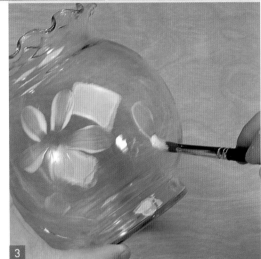

5 ▪ Paint Flowers Around the Vase

Continue to paint flowers until you have painted all around the vase. Stagger the placement of the flowers slightly.

6 ▪ Fill in the Center of Each Flower

With the gold outliner, start at the center of each flower and draw a spiral with the paint. You may want to practice on your palette first to get the feel for the pressure needed to squeeze the paint onto your surface. Do not worry about a perfect circle. The squiggly design evens out any bobbles.

7 ▪ Outline the Sides of Each Petal

Outline each petal in two steps. Starting at the center of the flower, draw a squiggly line following the curve of the petal with the gold outliner until you reach the top of the petal.

8 ▪ Finish the Outlining

Starting again at the flower center, draw a squiggly line along the other side of the petal until it meets the first line in the center. The squiggly lines can be on slightly different curves and still look good. Continue until you have outlined all the flower petals.

tip Remember, each flower is unique and your flower will look better for its unique character!

9 ▪ Add More Lines to Embellish

With the gold outliner, draw one or two curved lines from the flower center going up into each petal. These are shaped like parentheses. Continue until you have completed all the flowers.

Heat Set Your Glass Paint ▪ TO MAKE YOUR GLASS PAINT more permanent, allow the paint to dry for a minimum of twenty-four hours and bake it in a standard oven according to the directions on the paint bottle. The paint will be dishwasher resistant which means that you should be gentle when washing.

More Interesting Surfaces to Decorate With Paint

Once you learn the basics of painting, you can apply these skills to virtually any surface.

• RECYCLE OLD FURNITURE. Be sure to clean the surface well with TSP (be sure to do this in a well-ventilated area while wearing gloves) and sand lightly. Apply a coat of primer (available from home improvement stores), then paint the surface with latex or acrylic paint. Using what you learned in the Whimsical Painted Box project, you can paint vines and leaves with or without the rosebuds.

• OLD ROLLER SHADES make a terrific—and unexpected—surface. Brighten up any room with a painted shade.

• PRACTICE YOUR NEW SKILLS on cardstock to make greeting cards, bookmarks and gift tags.

variation

[**MATCHING CHAMPAGNE FLUTES**] For something different, try painting on glass champagne flutes. They are fast to paint and make beautiful keepsakes when painted in pairs.

collage & découpage
creative patchworks

*W*hat's not to love about collage? There is no need to stay inside the lines, no one "right" answer and tearing is as good (if not better!) than cutting. Approach it as a creative playtime with shapes, colors and texture. Dive in and trust that beautiful things will come of it. If you have a stash of pretty papers, pictures and other neat odds-and-ends accumulated, collage and découpage are definitely for you!

CREATIVITY SESSION: *Begin at the Beginning*

[CREATIVE BLOCK]

I'll never learn all the techniques of a craft that I need, so I never get started. I'll have to wait until I learn a lot more before I'll be ready to begin something new.

PERFECTIONISM AS AN EXCUSE

If you are a person who is afraid to try something before you feel you know everything about it, you are probably a perfectionist. It is hard for you to start something new for fear you won't be able to meet your own high standards. As Maria Shriver writes in her book, *Ten Things I Wish I'd Known—Before I Went Out Into the Real World*, the problem with perfectionism is that "Perfectionism doesn't make you feel perfect. It makes you feel inadequate."

Perfectionism can become an excuse to justify procrastination. Why do something if it can't be done perfectly? There is a "normal" level of perfectionism but we have to be able to accept personal and situational limitations. It is good to want to do well but if we take our desire for perfection too far, it actually inhibits our ability to do our best.

It is crucial at this stage in your creative journey to give yourself permission to be a beginner. Julia Cameron, author of *The Artist's Way*, writes, "Progress, not perfection, is what we should be asking of ourselves." You cannot progress from "beginner" to "advanced" in any skill unless you are willing to be a beginner in the first place!

YOU DON'T HAVE TO KNOW IT ALL

Something that many people do not know about law school (and I can only speak for California, since that is where I went to school) is that students are taught what is called "common law." By the end of law school, students have studied many areas of law and their minds are full of references as to how law works generally. Because there are so many laws, the law is constantly changing, and many lawyers practice in more than one state and/or jurisdiction, knowing how to use the tools to find and understand the law is more important than knowing every law on the books.

Although I no longer practice law, this is one of the most powerful lessons of my education and I find it applies to virtually every area of my life. Knowledge is a powerful thing, but experience and the ability to learn are more important.

OVERCOME YOUR FEAR

One of the reasons for hiding behind the label of "perfectionist" is a fear of criticism about your efforts. (See chapter six for help on dealing with criticism.) Ultimately, you have to decide that finding your creative voice is worth the risk.

Even without all the knowledge you need (yet), you are an amazingly creative, adaptive and resourceful person. Imagine what is possible if you put your intention behind your desire to create. Your creative voice is waiting to burst into song (and we want to hear it!), but first you must begin.

collage & découpage: getting started

WITH THE CUT-AND-PASTE SKILLS YOU LEARNED IN KINDERGARTEN, YOU CAN CREATE UNIQUE AND CONTEMPORARY ARTWORK. Both collage and découpage use cut paper, but collage focuses on combining a variety of elements to create a compositional design. Collage and découpage require few supplies to get started. You will need good scissors, an adhesive such as a glue stick or Perfect Paper Adhesive, a bone folder to smooth flat your pieces once they are glued, and something on which to collage. You can use virtually any surface—blank journal covers, lampshades, boxes, picture frames—anything that can be pasted upon. Just be sure to buy an adhesive appropriate for the surface you choose. Some adhesives work better than others on non-porous surfaces such as glass, metal or plastic.

You can embellish your pieces with hand-lettered words and phrases. If you are working on a dark surface, use a light-colored pen such as a gel pen or white Zig Opaque Writer to make your words stand out.

In this chapter, I have used elements from companies that create color sheets for the purpose of collage and prepasted cutouts for découpage. This way, you can recreate my designs if you wish to do so. However, you may enjoy creating similar projects by using magazine ads, clip art and color copies of photos or actual objects such as keys, letters and old lace that you have at home.

confidence builders

✳ DESIGN SURPRISE

Découpage and collage are excellent crafts to build your design confidence. As with rubber stamping, you can use preexisting elements to create something wholly new. In other words, you don't have to know how to draw or paint or create things perfectly. The joy of collage is that you can make your artwork very personal by including items from your life. Collage and découpage also help you to learn basic design and layout skills.

Make color photocopies of pictures and ephemera from your life (see the sidebar on page 48 for examples) and challenge yourself to create as many unique designs as you can with the same elements. You may be surprised that the same shapes and colors can be combined to create dozens of unique designs.

exercise: playing with composition

There is no "right" way to compose a collage. Start by placing pieces around your cover and rearranging until you find a design you like.

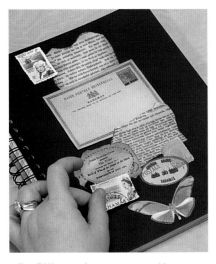

▪ **Try Different Arrangements** You might choose to arrange the elements down the center of your book cover as shown here.

▪ **Create a Focal Point** You might choose to use fewer elements, concentrating on one or two larger pieces. Note how the brightness of the globe element stands out compared to the color of the other elements shown. It is important to pay attention to both shape and color when putting your collage together.

▪ **Make Interesting Patterns** Here I chose to use a mix of one large piece with several complementary medium and small elements in a diagonal slant across the cover. Try to arrange your collage elements so that the different shapes and sizes make an interesting pattern against the background.

✳ make a travel journal collage

The next time you go on a trip, save all of the ephemera you pick up while traveling. This might include items such as ticket stubs, maps, stamps or pictures from a travel brochure. When pasted on a journal cover, simple items such as these transform a plain book into one that makes you want to open it to see what is inside! This project makes a wonderful gift for a friend's vacation or keepsake for your own travel memories.

✳ mistakes as opportunities

I was once in a class where a student painted a section with the "wrong" color. The teacher came over and said, "That isn't a mistake. It is a design opportunity!" The word "mistake" assumes that there is only one way to do something; that is rarely the case in creative pursuits. Some of the best designs and most innovative inventions have come from "mistakes."

One exciting aspect of "mistakes" is that they often occur when you are not paying full attention to what you are doing. When this happens, your subconscious mind takes over. Rather than considering the act an error, look at it as something with potential merit. You may be inspired to create something entirely new!

dragonfly journal

This charming book makes a great journal, scrapbook or photo album. Prepasted wallpaper cutouts make this project fast and fun! This blank book is an easy way to get your feet wet, creatively speaking. Even the greatest perfectionist can be satisfied with her work on this simple project.

MATERIALS

1 6" x 8" (15.2 x 20.3cm) mauve spiral-bound memory book

2 five dragonfly wallpaper cutouts

3 white opaque ink pen

4 scissors

5 sponge

6 bone folder

[optional]

7 wax palette

8 no. 20 brush

1 ▪ Arrange Your Wallpaper Cutouts

Choose several prepasted wallpaper cutouts that go well with the cover of your journal. Place several of the cutouts around the cover until you find a layout that you like. Allow the edges of your cutouts to flow off the edge of the journal for a more interesting design, keeping in mind that your design will have to stop short of the spiral binding.

2 ▪ Trim Off the Excess

With your cutouts in place, trim the excess off the pieces that will flow off the edge of your journal.

3 ▪ Moisten the Adhesive

With a damp (not wet) sponge, moisten the back of each cutout to reactivate the paste. Be sure to moisten the edges well so that the piece will adhere evenly. You may prefer to do this over a piece of paper or palette so that the paste is not trans-ferred to your table.

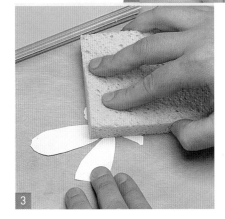

4 ▪ Paste Elements Into Place

Once each cutout is pasted into place, use a bone folder to smooth the paper down and remove bubbles and excess moisture. If you do not have a bone folder, you can use the flat side of a brush, a credit card or other smooth, flat object.

5 ▪ Embellish With Dotted Lines

After all the cutouts are in place, use the white opaque pen to draw dotted lines in front and behind each of the dragonflies in a curving design. The white dots tie the brightness of the wings into the darker background, giving it motion and visual interest.

tip Because the pen uses a thin paint-like ink, do a few test lines on scrap paper before writing on your project.

variation

[USING ONLY ONE IMAGE]

Découpaging a single beautiful image is sometimes all that is needed to transform a plain box into something special. Images like this magnolia can be cut from old magazines, gift wrap or wallpaper sample books.

Include Elements From Your Own Life

Collage and découpage can be made more personal by incorporating personal memorabilia into your designs. I keep plastic boxes filled with magazine clippings, found ephemera and personal keepsakes for use in my collages. Below are a few examples of things you might want to collect

• TICKET STUBS, RECEIPTS AND LAUNDRY TICKETS

• MOVIE REVIEWS (since newspaper is not acid-free, you should photocopy these items before using them in your art.)

• POSTCARDS AND SHIPPING TAGS

• OLD SLIDES AND PHOTOS

• NOTES AND LETTERS from friends and family

• STICKERS AND GAME PIECES

• USED POSTAGE

• PRESSED FLOWERS

• BEADS AND CHARMS (find them in gumball machines!)

• TWINE, RIBBON AND YARN

• CLIP ART from books or online sources

• USED TINSEL from last year's Christmas tree

You can also use photos to make interesting collage elements by photocopying color photos in black and white.

china album

A fun trend in scrapbooking is to create an album to document family china. China collectors also use these books to keep track of their patterns— where and when they found an item and how much they paid for it. If you like the look of a broken china mosaic, this collage can be adapted to other surfaces. You could even photocopy a plate and then cut it up to look like broken china if you have a pattern you particularly love.

◄ MATERIALS

1 preprinted china collage sheets (or color copies of actual china)

2 12" x 12" (30.5 x 30.5cm) navy blue spiral-bound memory book

3 craft glue or Perfect Paper Adhesive

4 white opaque ink pen

5 scissors

6 wax palette

7 no. 12 flat brush

[not shown]

8 cosmetic sponge

9 bone folder

10 ruler

1 ▪ Cut Out the Collage Elements

Carefully cut out the designs you want to use in your collage. With a collage sheet such as this one, you may want to cut out all of the designs and then select what will go into the final design after trying different combinations.

2 ▪ Create the Layout

Lay out the pieces in the pattern until you find a pleasing configuration. In this design, I decided to concentrate my pattern only on the edge. When you have the pieces organized the way you want them, you can either trace around each piece with a pencil or pick one piece up at a time to glue it into place. The tracing method is good if you are concerned that the pieces might be disturbed before you can glue them into place.

3 ▪ Apply Glue to Each Piece

Pour a pool of white craft glue or Perfect Paper Adhesive onto your palette. With a flat brush, apply a thin layer of glue to the back of each piece. Excess moisture is what causes paper to bubble, so apply the glue thinly.

4 ▪ Sponge Off Any Stray Glue

Use a cosmetic sponge to mop up any excess glue around the edges of your collage cutouts. Because you are not applying a top coat of varnish or adhesive over these pieces, you do not want the excess glue to soak into the album cover. This could darken the color of the paper in that spot.

Use Clip Art ▪ TRY BOOKSTORES AND LIBRARIES for copyright-free clip art books as a source for interesting images. Some books include images on CD-ROM so that you can print them from your computer. This gives you the ability to resize, color and otherwise change the images as you desire. There are also online resources for clip art. Be sure the Web site specifies "copyright free" before using any image from an online source.

5 ▪ Smooth Down the Edges

With a bone folder or other smooth, flat object such as this plastic chisel, smooth any bubbles out of each piece. Make sure that the edges of the papers are glued down so they will not catch and rip later.

6 ▪ Embellish the Design With Markers

With the white opaque ink pen, draw a pair of dashed lines along the inside edge of the china mosaic design. I made my dashes slightly curved and added dots in between to draw attention away from the fact that the edge of the pattern was not perfectly straight.

7 ▪ Draw the Baseline for the Title

Use a ruler to draw a straight line across the cover where you will place your text. Use a light hand with the pencil so it can be easily erased and does not make an indentation on the cover.

tip You will find that it looks better if you place the title of your journal slightly above or below the center of the book.

8 ▪ Write the Title on the Album Cover

Lightly sketch in the book title with a pencil. Pay attention to the spacing and letter size. When you are happy with the lettering, use a white opaque ink pen to ink in the title. Because the pen uses a thick paint-like ink, you will want to do a few test lines on scrap paper before writing on your project.

tip If you don't like your handwriting, consider using an alphabet stencil (available from craft stores) to trace on the words or refer to the sample alphabet on page 53 for inspiration.

9 ▪ Add the Final Embellishments

To give the title greater weight and visual interest on the dark book cover, I have embellished the "F" and "C" with a few extra lines and dots and underlined the rest of the title. This is a good way to cover up any bobbles in your handwriting!

10 ▪ Erase Stray Pencil Lines

After giving the ink a few minutes to set, erase any visible pencil lines.

Copying Tip ▪ BE CAREFUL

when photocopying artwork unless it specifies that it is copyright free or you have direct permission from the artist or owner of the image. It is generally safe to use clippings cut directly (not photocopied) from magazines if you use them for your personal use only.

✳ where to find your collage muses

✳ *Many Internet groups and Web sites* celebrate the use of collage. You can even purchase assorted ephemera and old photographs to use in your collages. Use your favorite Internet search engine to search for the term "collage." You can find discussion groups at groups.yahoo.com and www.topica.com.

✳ *A couple of step-by-step project books* that may interest you include: Collage Art: A Step-by-Step Guide and Showcase by Jennifer L. Atkinson (Quarry Books) and Creative Collage Techniques by Nita Leland and Virginia Lee Williams (North Light Books).

✳ *The Web site collageart.org* is a great informational site about collage and collage artists.

✳ *Jonathon Talbot* is a well-known teacher and author on the subject of collage. His Web site recommends books and resource information. Visit him at www.talbot1.com.

✳ *Get inspired by visiting GlobalCollage.com,* an amazing Web site that shows you a new collage every thirty seconds. See the collages at www.globalcollage.com/new_site/collage_index.html.

✳ *Claudine Hellmuth* is a collage artist and product developer who has set a new standard in collage. Visit her Web site at www.collageartist.com.

✳ *Art-e-zine* is an British online magazine about collage and stamping arts at www.art-e-zine.co.uk/contents.html.

tips on good lettering

A fun way to personalize your collage and découpage designs is to incorporate lettering. There are many books and classes to help you learn traditional lettering and calligraphy arts. However, your own printing or handwriting can work as well. Here are a couple of tips to get you started.

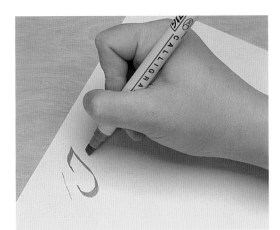

Using a Calligraphy Pen

When using a calligraphy marker, hold the pen nib or tip turned at a 45° angle to the baseline on which you are writing. This will naturally give you the wide and narrow lines that are the hallmark of basic calligraphy.

Hand-Lettering Your Work

Use markers in festive colors to incorporate lettering into your design. Be sure to first draw a light line with a pencil and ruler so that the writing does not slant. If you are not confident about your writing, trace the words lightly in pencil first. When your lettering is complete, simply erase the pencil marks.

Use this simple handwritten alphabet below as a guide to creating your own hand-lettered works. (You have permission to photocopy and resize this alphabet if you wish.)

Aa Bb Cc Dd Ee
Ff Gg Hh Ii Jj Kk
Ll Mm Nn Oo Pp
Qq Rr Ss Tt Uu
Vv Ww Xx Yy Zz

1234567890

Simple Cursive

bookmaking
turning over a new leaf

*I*n this age of mass production, creating your own hand-bound books is a simple pleasure. The practical nature of bookmaking only enhances its creative rewards. Their blank pages and attractive covers will quickly inspire you to find original ways to use and embellish them. Fill yours with inspirations, projects you want to try, and images to spur your creativity.

CREATIVITY SESSION: *When the Well Goes Dry*

[CREATIVE BLOCK]

I get started on a project and then I just go blank. I feel like the well is dry and no matter what I do, I can't figure out how to finish the project. I know it isn't right, but I don't know how to fix it.

HAVING A VISION

"Artist's block" may never hit you, or you may deal with it on an ongoing basis. There are many reasons for this type of block. It could be fear or your inner critic; it might be boredom or it could be that you simply aren't inspired with your current plans.

It is hard to be inspired if you don't have a clear vision of what you are trying to accomplish. If you decide you want to go on a trip, for example, it is hard to pack unless you know whether you are going to Alaska or Florida, right? Similarly, we have to have a vision of what we are trying to accomplish creatively in order to get ourselves moving.

One way to handle this is to think (or preferably write in a journal) about why you want to be creative. What does it give you? What would it give you if you devoted yourself to it in the way you would like? Do you have a long-term goal? Do you want to write books, teach or own a store? Do you just want to feel like you have become the best _____ (insert art form here, e.g., painter, mosaic artist, etc.) that you can be? When you are clear about what you want, it is easier to get yourself to work toward it.

If the ranting of your inner critic is bothering you, go to the index in this book and look for the specific issues related to this topic covered in earlier chapters. The best way to deal with an inner critic problem is to start working. If I am really procrastinating about work, I force myself to work on a project and set a timer for forty-five minutes. That is long enough to accomplish something, yet not so long that it is overwhelming. The first step is often the hardest. Working for a short chunk of time makes it easier. See the list on page 56 for more ideas on getting yourself moving.

BREAK YOUR PROJECTS DOWN

Becoming overwhelmed can also cause blocks. When we are about to start a project, we tend to look at the big picture (or finished project) which can overwhelm us. As we think of all we have to do, that leads to thoughts of even more things that need to be done and suddenly we are paralyzed by the thought of starting the project.

The best cure for this creative block is to break the project down into a series of steps and concentrate on the first one. Start by creating a list of what you will need to do. Reorganize the list by grouping similar items together. Next, prioritize the list by importance and urgency. Finally, choose one item on the list and get started.

It can take self-discipline to let go of the big picture. Being overwhelmed is a strong emotion. At this point, you might want to go back to the success list you created in chapter two. When you compare your current situation to some of the true challenges in your life, you will remember just how strong you are.

bookmaking:
getting started

WHILE THERE ARE DOZENS OF DIFFERENT WAYS TO BIND PAGES BETWEEN TWO COVERS TO FORM A BOOK, YOU ONLY NEED TO LEARN ONE OF THEM TO DISCOVER THE PLEASURES OF MAKING YOUR OWN BOOKS BY HAND.

The projects in this chapter use an easy-to-make design called an accordion book. This simple book has a single long, accordion-pleated sheet inside that folds out to form a perfect space for writing notes, pasting keepsakes and sending snapshots to a friend.

The best book covers are made from binder's board: a sturdy, acid-free board ideal for covers. If you can't find binder's board, you can substitute any medium-weight cardboard, such as the kind found on the back of a paper tablet. You will need large sheets of paper for the inside pages. Wrap your cover boards with your favorite decorative paper. Handmade papers are especially good for this because they are strong and flexible.

Trim large sheets of paper with a craft knife, a good ruler and a cutting mat. For smaller papers, use scissors or a paper trimmer. To make your book last, use an acid-free glue with a low moisture content to keep the paper from buckling. A glue stick or thin layer of white craft glue also works well.

Finally, decorative elements such as rubber stamps, ink, decorative beads and buttons, collage elements, ribbon or art fibers make each book personal and unique.

Materials such as these decorative papers are perfect for decorating book covers.

confidence builders

✳ PRIMING THE PUMP

Our lives are often so hectic and demanding that we simply have nothing left for our creativity. When I am feeling blocked and cranky about doing something creative, I do what I call "priming the pump." (Have you ever had to pump a spray bottle several times before the fluid will flow? That is priming the pump.)

When I am feeling creatively wrung out, I know I must make time for me. Here are some ideas of things I do that might help you:

- Clean and reorganize your workspace. It can be very inspiring to touch all those art supplies and remember why you bought them!
- Write down your project as a question, for example, how can I do _____ and make it fun? Write your thoughts down—even the crazy ideas. Put it away and read it the next day. Underline ideas that sound plausible and make plans to use them.

- Do something new. Turn the music on loud and dance. Paint your wall. Go to the park or mall and people watch. Bring a sketchbook and sketch without the need to be perfect. Buy a temporary tattoo and wear it all day.
- Switch mediums. If you normally paint, try creating a project in mosaic or paper. Try paper instead of tile. Looking at something from a new angle is always educational and inspiring.
- Go on to the next thing on your list. If what you are doing is not inspiring, it may be hard to finish it. Give yourself permission to have some unfinished projects. Find other crafters and artists and have an "unfinished project" swap. You may see unending possibilities in another artist's unfinished work.

lock & key book

Combine the rubber stamping skills learned in chapter two with basic bookmaking techniques to create this simple and practical accordion book. Although I am using art papers for this book, you can use less expensive papers and create your own patterned paper with stamps or stencils.

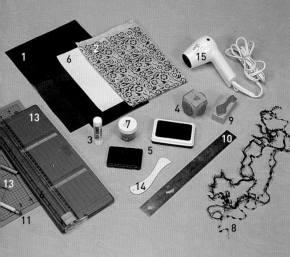

MATERIALS

1 20" x 40" (50.8 x 101.6cm) sheet of black text-weight paper

2 large sheet of black and cream patterned paper (or design of your choice)

3 glue stick

4 keyhole rubber stamp (JudiKins)

5 black embossing ink pad

6 8½" x 11" (21.6 x 28cm) sheet of cream-colored cardstock

7 black embossing powder

8 black art fibers or ribbon

9 old key or key stamp

10 cork-backed ruler

11 pencil

12 cutting mat and craft knife

13 scissors or paper trimmer

14 bone folder

15 embossing or heat gun

[not shown]

16 two pieces of binder's board cut to 4½" x 5¾" (11.4 x 14.6cm)

17 rubber brayer

1 ▪ Measure and Cut the Inside Pages

The inside pages of this book use a simple accordion fold: a long strip of paper that is folded back and forth to form an accordion pleat. For the pages of this book, cut a long strip measuring 5½" x 25½" (13.9 x 64.8cm) from the large sheet of black paper.

tip Because you are measuring several pieces of paper to create this book, measure carefully before cutting your paper.

2 ▪ Measure and Score the Folds

The six accordion panels are each 4¼" (10.8cm) wide. Carefully measure the folds across the paper, and then score them by running the edge of a bone folder along the line. Use a ruler as a guide to keep the lines straight.

3 ▪ Accordion Fold the Panels

Once the lines are scored, fold the paper back and forth into an accordion pattern and crease the folds into place using a bone folder or other hard, smooth tool.

4 ▪ Cut the Cover Boards and Paper

Measure and cut two pieces of binder's board to 4½" x 5¾" (11.4 x 14.6cm). If you cannot find binder's board, a good substitute is the stiff cardboard from the back of a paper tablet.

Measure and cut two pieces of patterned paper so that they stick out generously beyond the edges of the cardboard pieces. With a glue stick, apply adhesive over the entire surface of one side of the cardboard.

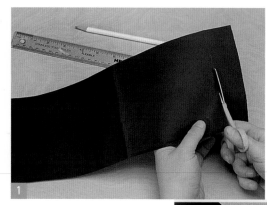

Gluing Tip •

IF YOU LIVE in an area that is very dry, glue sticks may not hold indefinitely. If this is a problem for you, use Perfect Paper Adhesive or other acid-free glue.

5 ▪ Smooth the Paper Over the Covers

Use a rubber brayer or other soft, smooth tool to smooth the paper into place over the adhesive. Because this paper is very lightweight, a harder tool such as a bone folder might rip the paper.

tip If you don't have a rubber brayer, place another sheet of paper over the first and use it to protect the bottom sheet while smoothing out the bubbles.

6 ▪ Trim the Cover Paper

Trim the paper to between ½ inch and ¾ inch (1.3 and 2cm) around the cardboard. Cut off corner notches on all four corners of the piece.

7 ▪ Glue the Flaps

Apply the glue stick to the paper flaps and fold them over onto the cardboard around all four sides. Smooth with a brayer to make sure the flaps are thoroughly glued into place.

✳ creative networking

Find a local group or an online group to talk to about your creative work. Check out local bookstores, art stores and churches to find nearby craft or artist groups. There are few things more inspiring than being with someone who is passionate about their work. Taking a class, making a call or just spending time with people who are not blocked can get you working again.

8 ▪ Ink and Stamp a Keyhole Design

Ink a keyhole stamp using a black embossing ink pad (not dye ink). Stamp the design
onto a scrap of cream-colored cardstock.

tip Try not to rock the stamp as you
apply it to the surface or you will get a
blurred image.

9 ▪ Pour on Embossing Powder

Over a clean piece of scrap paper, apply a
generous amount of black embossing
powder onto the stamped design. Hold
the paper at an angle and tap off any
excess powder onto the scrap paper. Use
the scrap paper to return any unused
powder to your embossing powder jar.

10 ▪ Heat the Image With an Embossing Gun

With an embossing gun, gently heat the
ink and powder. Continuously move the
heat gun in small circles so as not to burn
the paper. As the powder heats, you will
see it develop a smooth, satiny sheen.
Once the embossed image is cool and
hard, trim around the stamped design.

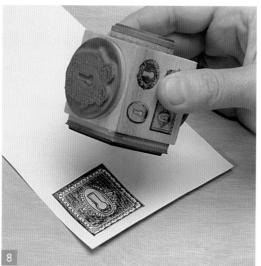

✳ making a change

*The projects in this chapter take advantage of the wide variety of handmade and
printed papers currently available at arts and craft stores. Challenge yourself
by changing the designs with different paper than those used in the project.*

*From tissue paper to plastics, the options are endless and making a small
change will help you see the project in a new way. Instead of the keyhole
stamp used in the Lock and Key Book, try using a stamp you already own.
Making little changes to book designs is the first step to expanding your own
design skills.*

11 ▪ Glue the Keyhole to the Cover

Measure and cut a narrow strip of black paper to 5¾" x 1" (14.6 x 2.5cm). With a glue stick, glue the strip of paper in about ½" (1.3cm) from the left edge of the front cover. Next, glue the embossed keyhole design on top of it, using the photo as a guide .

12 ▪ Glue the Book Ties to the Covers

Cut black art fibers into two sixteen-inch (40.6cm) strands to make ties to close the book. If you prefer, use thin ribbon or yarn. With a glue stick, glue one strand to the inside of the front cover as if coming out of the left side (as you look down on the piece to glue it). Glue the other strand coming from the right side of the back cover (just as you see in the photo).

13 ▪ Glue the Pages Inside the Covers

Glue each end of the black accordion panel into the book covers using the glue stick. Pay particular attention to the edges of the piece so they do not lift and tear later. The black paper will cover the fibers and inside surface of the covers.

tip Before gluing, place the pages inside the covers first to be sure they are oriented properly and you know which side of the paper to glue.

14 ▪ Add a Key to Finish the Book

When the glue has dried, wrap the fibers around the book to tie the book shut. As a finishing touch, I have added an old key, purchased at a thrift store, to the end of one of the strings.

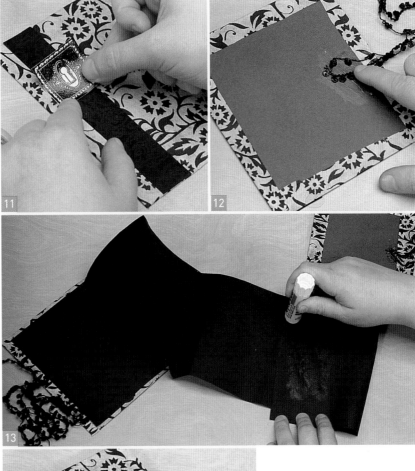

umbrella book

Challenge yourself by using elements that are "out of context" in your creative work. This cheerful umbrella reminded me of the family vacations of my youth. I saved it until I found the perfect project for it.

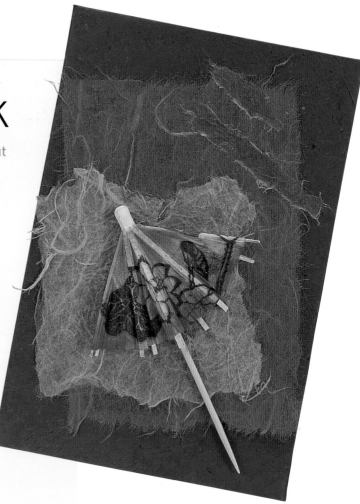

MATERIALS

1. decorative handmade papers in turquoise, yellow, azure, purple and fuchsia

2. two pieces of binder's board cut to 4" x 6" (10.2 x 15.2cm)

3. glue stick

4. novelty drink paper umbrella

5. pencil

6. craft knife

7. cork-backed ruler

8. scissors or paper trimmer

[not shown]

9. cutting mat

10. thick white craft glue (Aleene's Tacky Glue)

11. soft rubber brayer

[optional]

12. bone folder

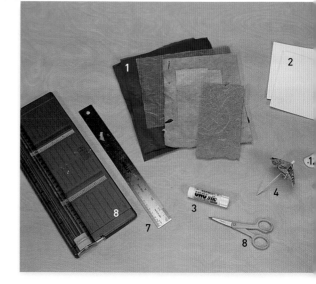

1 ▪ Trim and Glue the Cover Paper to the Boards

Measure and cut two pieces of azure blue paper to approximately 5" x 7" (12.7 x 17.8cm) and two pieces of binder's board to 4" x 6" (10.2 x 15.2cm). If you don't have binder's board, use medium-weight cardboard in its place.

Glue each board to the center of each paper with a glue stick. Use the brayer (or other smooth tool) to smooth the paper and make sure it is evenly adhered across the board.

2 ▪ Trim the Flaps and Glue It in Place

Cut off corner notches on all four sides of each piece. (Refer to step six of the Lock and Key Book on page 59.) Apply the glue stick to the paper flaps and fold them over onto the cardboard around all four sides. Smooth the paper with a brayer to make sure it is thoroughly glued into place.

3 ▪ Tear the Edges of the Fuchsia Paper

After cutting a piece of fuchsia paper to 5" x 4" (12.7 x 10.2cm), measure out a 4½"x 3" (11.4 x 7.6cm) rectangle on the piece with a ruler and a pencil. Place the cork-backed ruler along the line and tear the edges off. This gives the paper the uneven deckled look of handmade paper.

tip If the paper is difficult to tear, moisten along the line with a cotton swab dampened with water.

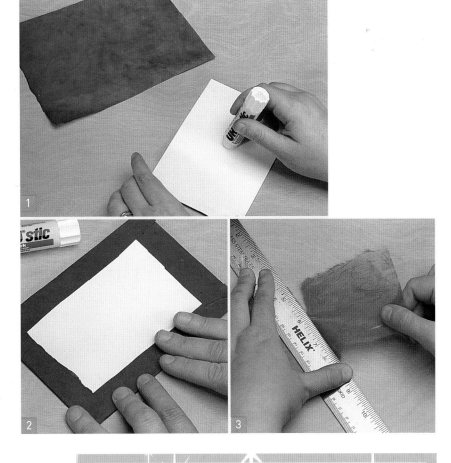

✳ adding personal symbols

Consider developing a personal symbol to include in all of your artwork. When I do illustration work, I use a simple image of one of my cats. It has become a creative challenge to work the cat into every picture—sometimes as a feature and sometimes unobtrusively. (He was once featured as a slightly misshapen flower in a vase.) Your symbol might be something as simple as a circle or a swirl, or something much more complex. Look at your artwork to see if there are already symbols that show up on a regular basis. When I paint, I like to include graceful swirls. What images show up— or will show up—in your work?

4 ▪ Tear and Glue Turquoise Paper

Using the same technique, measure and tear the edges off the turquoise paper to approximately 2¾" x 2¾" (7 x 7cm). Don't worry about making the lines straight. The torn edges add texture to the cover design.

Glue the fuchsia and turquoise papers to one of the covers with a glue stick. Use a brayer or other smoothing tool to make sure all of the edges are fully adhered. Finally, add a few torn strips of purple paper to the upper right corner. Refer to the photo on page 62 for placement.

5 ▪ Cut the Brackets in the Umbrella

Cut out the support brackets inside one side of the umbrella. This will enable you to the fold umbrella in half (while in the open position) without ripping it. Before cutting and folding the umbrella, look at its design so that you can position the part you like best on the front of the book.

6 ▪ Apply Glue to the Inside of the Umbrella

Apply a thick white craft glue to the inside of the umbrella to hold it closed. When it is dry, apply more glue to the back of the umbrella and along the toothpick handle.

7 ▪ Position the Umbrella in Place

Carefully position the umbrella in place. The thickness of this glue will hold the umbrella in place as it dries. To finish the book, follow the directions in the Lock and Key Book to cut and fold bright yellow accordion pages. Trim your paper to 22½" x 5¾" (57.2 x 14.6cm) and fold each panel 3¾" (9.5cm) wide.

tip I chose yellow paper for my book, but any bright, contrasting color will match the cheerful design of this cover.

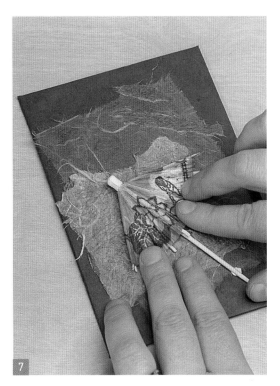

Fun Things to Do with Handmade Books

- TURN YOUR BOOK into a thank-you gift by filling it with photos and keepsakes on each page.

- USE THE BOOK as unique stationery for special occasions, such as a letter of congratulations for a graduation or new baby.

- COMMEMORATE A PARTY or create a small keepsake for a trip by filling your pages with snapshots from an instant camera, such as a Polaroid JoyCam or i-Zone.

- CREATE A BOOK with your children's or grandchildren's feet and handprints on the pages. Make notes about their personalities and favorite things at specific times in their lives.

- COMMEMORATE SPECIAL TIMES in your own life. Create a book with nine pages with a photograph of each month of your pregnancy. Create a book about moving day to a new house or apartment.

- CREATE A SPECIAL GIFT by filling each page of the book with notes about the things you admire about each of your friends and family members.

- FILL A BOOK with ideas for beating artist's block so that the next time you experience it, you will remember what worked to overcome it!

✳ where to find muses to inspire you further

✳ *You can find inspiration* and take in-depth classes in book arts at the Chicago Center for Book and Paper Arts (www.bookandpaper. org/index.html) and the San Francisco Center for the Book (www.sfcb.org).

✳ *Look for bookmaking supplies* at your local craft, art or rubber stamp store. If you have trouble finding supplies, try searching for online resources such as Talas: at www.talas-nyc.com and Volcano Book Arts at www.volcanobookarts.com.

✳ *Two good books* for beginners are The Essential Guide to Making Handmade Books by Gabrielle Fox (North Light Books) and Making Books by Hand: A Step-by-Step Guide by Mary McCarthy and Phillip Manna (Quarry Books).

papermaking
breaking the mold

*I*f the prospect of sharing your creative efforts with others both thrills you and fills you with anxiety, consider papermaking. While your friends and family may not be interested in unusual artwork, paper makes the perfect gift because it's something everyone uses and understands. Papermaking projects also allow you to explore brilliant colors, exotic materials and interesting textures—and every piece you make is unique!

CREATIVITY SESSION: *Dealing With Criticism*

[CREATIVE BLOCK]

I'm afraid of what people will think if I claim to be creative or an artist. I'll appear stupid or foolish to my friends and family.

THE POWER OF CRITICISM

When you first begin your creative journey, criticism can be devastating. Your creative confidence may be fragile and criticism may echo your inner fears and discourage you from moving forward. Indeed, it may have been criticism as a child that prevented you from seeking your creative path sooner.

I do not mean to say that criticism can never be a positive thing. In many cases, a well-intentioned comment can be invaluable. So it is important to learn to decide for yourself when criticism is justified and helpful, and when it is simply manipulative or derogatory. You can do this by analyzing two aspects of criticism: the comment itself and the motivation of the person making the comment.

THE DISPARAGING COMMENT

If someone says something derogatory about your work, it is generally intended to make you react in a certain way. Perhaps what you are doing makes them uncomfortable. Maybe they believe that there is just one pie of success and if you have a slice, they can't have it. Maybe your creative dedication is making them feel bad because it reminds them of what they wish they could be doing. Do you see the pattern? The comment is all about their feelings. It isn't about you.

Sometimes a disapproving statement comes from the "right place." People may believe that they are protecting you by telling you the truth (or at least their version of it) so that you will not be rejected or embarrassed when you share your work. When I first started my brightly colored designs, for example, well-meaning friends pointed out that a more neutral palette was in style at the time. They weren't trying to discourage me; they thought that the change would help me sell my work. They did not understand that the unusual color palette set me apart from other artists and ultimately launched my career because it was unique.

SIFTING THROUGH SUGGESTIONS

It is important that you be protective of your work and your creative ego. If you let the opinion of every person in your life affect you, you will never get much done. As the saying goes, "You can't please everyone." Be discriminating about the people whose opinion you give power over you and your work.

Don't take all criticism to heart. At the same time, don't automatically dismiss it. You may find that a comment from the most unlikely source may provide a valuable new perspective. Difficult as it may be, let go of the negativity and embrace the opportunity for improvement.

Trust your instinct. If the comment resonates with you, it may be that it touches on an old insecurity. It may also be something that brings about a new way of thinking. Decide whether the comment has merit, then act on it or let it go. Remember that what others say does not change who you are unless you let it.

papermaking: getting started

ONE OF THE BEST THINGS ABOUT HANDMADE PAPER IS THAT THERE IS NO "RIGHT" WAY IT SHOULD LOOK. Each piece will have its own unique character and each will be equally beautiful. If you use the same materials in the same amounts with the same equipment I used in this book, the pieces will still be different. There is tremendous freedom in knowing there is "no right way" paper should look; it means that you cannot do it wrong.

Papermaking is an extremely economical craft because if you don't like the finished result, you can throw it back into the blender and try again! Traditionally, papermaking was a messy business. New kits, such as the Papyrus 21 Handmade Papermaking Kit I use in this chapter, make trying papermaking on a smaller scale simpler and easier.

To get started in papermaking, you will need a papermaking kit, access to water, a large supply of paper towels (or other absorbent cloth), a craft knife and cutting surface, art fibers or ribbon, pulp or copy paper, a sponge, a blender (for papermaking use only), inclusions and decorative accessories such as brads to embellish your handmade paper.

I have a spare bathroom that I use when making paper because all of the water necessary to create the slurry can be messy. The papermaking kits use far less water (because they create smaller sheets of paper), but you will still need access to a sink and drainage area. For this reason, many paper artists like to work outside when they are creating larger sheets of paper.

confidence builders

* PROTECT YOURSELF

The fear of criticism can often be worse than the comment itself. Make a list of the things you think friends and family might say if they saw your art. (Include the person's name and the imaginary or real comment.) For each comment, imagine that your child (or grandchild or niece or nephew) told you that someone had said that to them. How would you respond? What would you say in their defense? What would you tell them about someone who would make that kind of comment? Are you not worthy of the same level of protection and defense?

Make a list of people you know who might be encouraging to you. What would they say? Consider bringing an example (or photos) of your work to them. Start by telling them that you are feeling a bit insecure and you could use someone to encourage you. It is okay to ask for what you need.

* GIFTS

If you are concerned about showing your friends and family your creative efforts, choose practical craft projects and give them as gifts. The book and gift tags are excellent examples of projects you could use to share your creativity in a practical way.

starry book

This unique book is an excellent gift or keepsake. If you try this craft and enjoy it, you can make the paper for the inside of the book as well as the covers! Just remember to use less paper pulp if you want the inside pages to be thinner than the covers.

MATERIALS

1 two sheets of plain white copier paper

2 dried violet petals

3 star-shaped brads

4 six sheets of light green or yellow paper cut to 5½" x 3½" (14 x 9cm)

5 ribbon, yarn or art fibers

6 blender

7 handmade papermaking kit

8 sponge

9 ¼" (6mm) hole punch

10 pencil

11 scissors

[not shown]

12 paper towels

13 craft knife

14 ruler

[additional materials for the heart shaped gift tag on page 76]

15 pop-up sponge

16 3" (7.6 cm) heart- or star-shaped cookie cutter

17 plastic opal flakes or glitter

Use a Paper-Only Blender • A BLENDER

should not be used for food after use with paper. Inexpensive blenders are available through discount department stores or you can find them through thrift shops.

1 ▪ Tear the Paper
Fill the blender with about 32 oz. (960 ml) of water. Tear up two sheets of white copier paper into small pieces and add it to the blender. This will make enough pulp to make a pair of fairly firm book covers.

2 ▪ Blend the Paper
Pulse the blender for several twenty-second bursts until the paper pulp is smooth with no large lumps or chunks of paper appearing.

3 ▪ Add Inclusions
To make your paper more interesting, you can add a wide variety of inclusions, such as glitter and flower petals, to the pulp. For this paper, I have chosen to blend dried violet petals into the mix so that they become part of the paper. Add a generous handful of petals to the blender.

Making Smear-Proof Paper • IF YOU PLAN to draw or write on your finished handmade paper, you will want to add sizing to your paper mixture. Sizing is a starchy solution that prevents inks from bleeding or smearing when you write on the finished paper. If you are using commercial paper to make your pulp, you do not need to add sizing—it's already in the paper. If you choose to use unsized paper pulp, you may want to add a commercial sizing or Perfect Paper Adhesive, which is available at many craft and art stores.

4 ▪ Blend in the Inclusions

Pulse the mixture in a series of twenty-second bursts until the inclusions are thoroughly blended throughout the mixture. The watery paper mixture is called slurry. It should be roughly the consistency of very thin oatmeal with no obvious lumps. The thicker the slurry, the thicker your finished paper will be. Add water to thin the mixture or add more paper to thicken.

5 ▪ Pour the Slurry Onto the Mold

Assemble the papermaking kit according to the instructions. You will have a vat, a mold and a deckle to start. The vat is the bottom basin in which the excess water and slurry goes. The mold is the flat screen on which the sheet of paper is formed. The deckle is the removable frame around the mold that holds the slurry in place.

Pour the slurry into the mold and deckle until it is about three-quarters full. You can rock the slurry slightly or stir it with your finger to even the surface.

6 ▪ Drain the Water

Lift the mold and deckle out of the vat, tilting it slightly to drain the water. Place the mold onto the upper rim of the vat. The rim holds the mold above the vat so when you apply a top screen any excess water drains directly into the vat.

72

7 ▪ Add a Top Screen Over the Paper

Place a screen on top of the slurry in the mold and deckle. The screen will protect and hold the paper sheet in place while you squeeze out the excess water.

8 ▪ Squeeze Out the Excess Water

With both hands, firmly press down on the screen. The more water you remove at this stage, the better. I like to pick up the deckle frame and press the screen down to get better leverage.

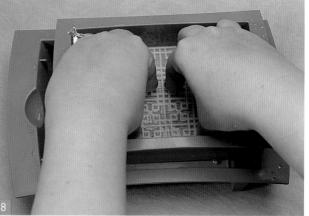

9 ▪ Prepare the Couch Cloth

Spread out a few layers of paper towels to absorb the moisture. Atop this stack, place the couch cloth provided in the kit. This cloth is a very absorbent type of paper that aids in removing excess water but does not grab and tear the paper.

tip This will take quite a few paper towels, so have plenty on hand. In place of paper towels, another option is to use a smooth fabric diaper or other absorbent cloth.

10 ▪ Remove the Top Screen

Gently remove the upper screen. Try to do
this carefully so that you don't lift pulp off
the paper which can result in a gouge.

11 ▪ Place the New Paper on the Towels

Place the mold and newly formed paper
down on the towels with the mold on top.
Press down again. You may find it helpful
to put a sponge over the mold so that
water is drawn out from both sides.
Remove the mold from the paper. Once
again, be gentle so as not to rip or gouge
the paper form.

tip If the paper still feels wet, place
paper towels and the couch cloth under
and over the paper form and press again.

12 ▪ Set Aside the Paper to Dry

Place the damp paper on a smooth surface
to dry. The paper will take on the form of
whatever is beneath it to some extent, so do
not put the paper on an uneven surface or
your paper will dry that way. You can speed
the drying time with a blow dryer or an iron.
Because of the thickness of the sheets, it
may take twenty-four to forty-eight hours to
dry thoroughly.

Don't forget: repeat steps one through
twelve to create a second sheet. When
your two sheets of paper are completely
dry, you are ready to create a book.

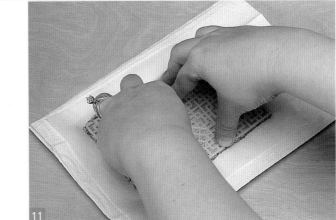

13 ▪ Punch the Holes for the Spine

The two sheets, placed lengthwise, will form the covers of your book. With a ruler and pencil, mark a spot ½" (1.3cm) in from one of the short edges and halfway down from the top. Mark the second sheet the same way. Punch over the pencil mark on each piece with a ¼" (6mm) round hole punch.

14 ▪ Make Notches on the Spine Edges

On the same side where the center hole was punched, mark the top and bottom edges above and below the center hole, ¾" (2cm) in from the edge.

With the hole punch, punch a half-circle notch ¾" (2cm) in from the edge on the top and bottom pencil marks. Do this for both cover sheets.

tip With a bone folder, you may wish to score a line connecting these two notches to allow the book to open more fully.

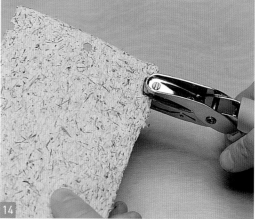

15 ▪ Decorate the Cover With Star-Shaped Brads

Embellish the front cover with five small, star-shaped brads. To do so, make a small cut in the front cover with a craft knife wherever you want to place a brad. Push a brad through each cut and spread the prongs open on the back to hold them in place.

tip If the book will get a lot of use, you can further secure the brads with a dab of glue.

16 ▪ Make the Pages

To make pages for the book, cut six sheets of green paper to 5½" x 3½" (14 x 9cm). Punch a hole in each sheet about ½" (1.3cm) in from the left edge and halfway down from the top.

Put the covers together with the paper sheets inside. Line up the holes and thread a 26" (66cm) length of art fiber or thin yarn through the hole. Leave about a 5" (13cm) loose "tail" in the front.

17 ▪ Wind Fibers Around the Book

The fibers will create the "binding" for the book. Holding the short end tight, wrap the long part of the fiber around the book until approximately 5" (13cm) remains. The ½" (1.3cm) notches cut on either side of the cover pieces will hold the wound fiber in place.

tip To keep your pages tight in the book, make sure that the fibers are taut and even on both sides of the book.

18 ▪ Tuck the End Through the Hole

When you are down to about 5" (13cm) left, poke the remaining thread through the center hole from the back of the book so that both ends come out of the center hole on the same side.

19 ▪ Tie the Ends to Secure the Pages

Wrap one end around the bundle of fibers now surrounding the book and tie it to the other end with a tight bow.

heart-shaped gift tag

The variety of cookie cutters available make creating shaped papers in a papermaking kit a simple process. The imperfections in the deckle edge (the uncut edge created where the paper meets the deckle and mold) make each piece unique.

You can also use this technique for party name tags, ornaments and more.

MATERIALS (Refer to the photo on page 70)

17 plastic opal flakes or glitter

16 3" (7.6cm) heart- or star-shaped cookie cutter

15 pop-up sponge

12 paper towels

11 scissors

9 ¼" (6mm) hole punch

7 handmade papermaking kit

6 blender

5 ribbon, yarn or art fibers

[not shown]

19 clear plastic or cling wrap

18 one sheet lavender copier paper

✴ exercise: inclusions

Inclusions and embedded items make paper unique. Gathering materials from your life can make your papermaking more personal. Make a project of finding inclusions from your life for use in your paper, for example leaves from your yard or walks, tinsel from last year's Christmas tree or frayed bits of yarn or fabric.

1 ▪ Trace the Cookie Cutter on a Sponge

Put a heart- or star-shaped cookie cutter down on a pop-up sponge and trace the inside of the shape with a pencil.

2 ▪ Cut Out the Sponge

Cut out the shape along the pencil line with scissors. Dampen the sponge to pop it up. Put the sponge aside for use later.

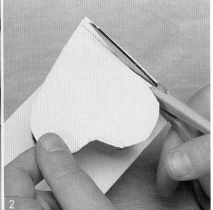

3 ▪ Add the Paper to the Blender

Pour 16 oz. (480 ml) of water into a blender you have dedicated exclusively to paper-making. Add between one-half to three-quarters of a sheet of torn lavender copier paper. Be sure the paper is torn into small pieces so that the blender will be able to break down the paper into pulp. Blend the paper in a series of twenty-second bursts until it creates a slurry that is smooth without any obvious chunks or lumps.

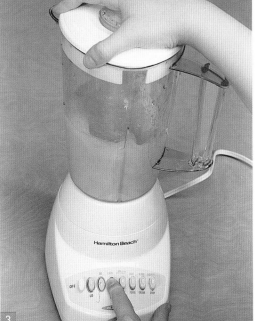

4 ▪ Pour the Slurry into the Cookie Cutter

Put the papermaking kit together follow-ing the instructions in the kit. (Each kit varies slightly.) Place the cookie cutter on the center of the mold. Pour the slurry mixture into the center of the cookie cut-ter until it is one-half to three-quarters full. The thicker you want the paper, the more slurry is needed.

5 ▪ Add the Opal Flakes

Sprinkle plastic opal flakes, glitter or other material additions over the slurry. The flakes need to sit on the top and soak into the slurry or they will flake off once the paper dries.

tip Adding the material at this point, rather than during the blending phase, embeds the materials on one side rather than throughout the paper. Choose which effect you like best.

6 ▪ Position the Sponge Over the Slurry

Put the mold up on the ledge of the vat to allow the water to drain. Because you don't have a screen the shape of the cookie cutter, you will use the heart-shaped sponge to press out the excess water. First, wrap a piece of plastic cling wrap over the bottom of the sponge. This will keep it from sticking to the wet fibers. Now place the sponge inside the cookie cutter.

7 ▪ Squeeze Out the Water

Squeeze the excess water out of the slurry by pressing down on the sponge evenly. Continue to press until the water stops dripping.

8 ▪ Place the Mold on the Couch Sheet

Place a stack of paper towels under a couch sheet. Lift the cookie cutter mold and press the paper out. Press down on the sponge to press out the water, and then remove the sponge. The clear plastic prevents the opal flakes from coming off as you press to remove the water.

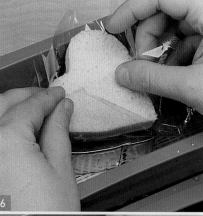

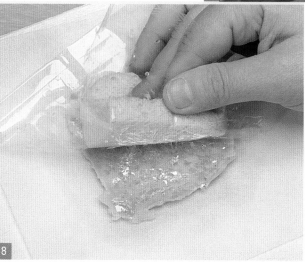

9 ▪ Press Out the Water

Place another stack of paper towels over the plastic. Press down evenly over the surface of the towels to further press out the water. Remove the towels, flip the paper over so that the plastic is on the bottom and set it on a flat surface to dry.

10 ▪ Punch a Hole to Hang

When the paper is thoroughly dry, carefully lift it from table. Some of the opal flakes will come off but most should be embedded into the paper. With a ¼" (6mm) hole punch, make a hole in the center of the "V" of the heart. Thread art fiber or ribbon through the hole.

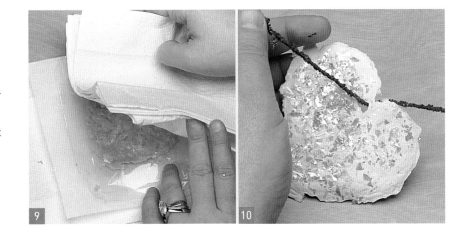

✳ places to go for inspiration

✳ **Papermaking Techniques Book:** Over 50 Techniques for Making and Embellishing Handmade Paper by John Plowman (North Light Books).

✳ **Arnold Grummer's Complete Guide to Easy Papermaking** by Arnold Grummer (Krause Publications).

✳ **Hand Papermaking, INC.** is a nonprofit group dedicated to keeping the art of papermaking alive (www.handpapermaking.org).

✳ **You can share** ideas with other papermaking artists through this online mailing list: groups.yahoo.com/group/papermaking.

✳ **Two great web sites** about papermaking and papier mâché are www.artfarm.com/papier.html and www.papermaking.net.

✳ **Peter Overpeck,** a handmade paper enthusiast, has an excellent informational Web site about papermaking history, techniques and more at www.overpeck.com.

More Ways to Use Handmade Paper

- MAKE PLACE CARDS for dinner with family and friends.
- USE YOUR PAPER FOR NAME TAGS for special events or meetings (just glue a pin on the back).
- ADD LOTS OF GLITTER for charming handmade ornaments for your tree.
- THE FEEL OF HANDMADE PAPER is distinctive and makes excellent business cards.
- CUT YOUR HANDMADE PAPER into strips to make unusual napkin rings. Join the rings with glue, decorative brads or sew with contrasting thread in large looping stitches.
- THE PAPERMAKING KIT shown makes postcard-sized pages. Decorate and use them for handmade holiday cards, moving announcements and other notes.
- MAKE YOUR PAPER EXTRA THICK and use it as a drink coaster. (Allow it to dry under a flat weight, such as a piece of glass or book, so the finished piece is level.)
- IF YOUR FIRST ATTEMPTS are thicker than you like, cut them into long strips and use them as bookmarks.

CHAPTER

7

metal & wire crafts
shining possibilities

o you remember as a child searching in the clouds to spot hidden shapes? Try the same thing with wire and metal. Twist a random coil, bend a scrap of wire mesh and inspire yourself to think up ways to transform everyday objects by embellishing them with metal. Metal is a beautiful and tremendously forgiving substance. If you don't like what you've made you can straighten it out and try again.

CREATIVITY SESSION: *Taking Control of Your Creativity*

[CREATIVE BLOCK]

I can never be creative because I never get any creative ideas. I know ideas are out there, but I have to wait for my "muse" to inspire me.

YOU DON'T HAVE TO WAIT

If you think the only creative people are those who have a muse or a direct line to inspiration, then it may be difficult for you to get started on your creative journey. The belief that we have to wait on inspiration may make us feel like we are out of control or separate from the process. If you believe that you don't happen to be one of the lucky few with a muse, this excuse might be a protection mechanism (and procrastination technique) you are using to avoid your fears.

I do not believe that there is a big vat full of creativity that is only ladled out from time to time to the elite. Creativity is our birthright. It is a gift that is given to each and every one of us. Creativity—the ability to create—is a skill we use every day. Learning to be more innovative in our approach and using it to expand our artistic ability is a matter of practice.

TIMING ISN'T EVERYTHING

There are certainly times we are more creative. If you have the flu or a cold, you aren't going to get a lot of quality creative time in. By the same token, you probably wouldn't be as good at housework or bowling during those times either. Your ability to be creative is not diminished when you are sick or tired or stressed, but your ability to tap into that creativity is dimmed for the present.

While there are certain things that sap our ability to be our creative best, there is no reason to give your creativity away by developing a belief system that says you can only be creative at certain times. Creativity is just problem solving. You solve problems nearly all day long from deciding what to eat for breakfast to making decisions at work to driving your car. You are always exercising your creativity. It is a never-ending fount. However, if you believe that you must wait for inspiration, then wait you will.

CLAIM YOUR POWER

Claim the power that is already inside you. Know that you are a creative being. Even if that voice has been told to "shush" for years, somewhere deep inside of you, it is there. Nothing is added to your life, nor do you get any points for humility or godliness by denying the gift of creativity inside you. Instead, claim that creativity every day. That is how to celebrate your life!

metal & wire crafts: getting started

WORKING WITH METAL IS WONDERFUL BECAUSE YOU CAN SHAPE IT (AND RESHAPE IT) INTO NEARLY ANYTHING. To that end, you can't do it wrong. Wire and craft metal, also called embossing metal, is readily available through craft stores in a variety of shapes, sizes and thicknesses. Because of its durability, you can shape and reshape most metal forms until you are happy with the final outcome. Wire is sold either plain or plastic-coated, like the Fun Wire used in this chapter, and in a variety of thicknesses or gauges. The higher the gauge number, the finer the wire. When you work with wire, don't be afraid to experiment with a variety of wire gauges and colors to see which ones create the best effect in your work. The two basic tools needed to work with wire are a good set of round-nose pliers (made for jewelry) and wire cutters. You can also shape or coil wire around items you already have at home, such as the handle of a paintbrush. Decorative extras such as beads, ribbons and stones are good to have handy as embellishments.

In addition to working with wire, try playing with sheets of embossing metal (available on a roll) and wire mesh (sold in folded sheets). The embossing metals come in copper, aluminum, brass and pewter. They are soft enough to be cut with scissors and can be textured or embossed with a stylus, brush handle or special embossing tools. Metal can also be aged with chemicals and paints made for that purpose.

confidence builders

* EXERCISE: MAKE IT EASY ON YOURSELF

Create a creative space all your own. Even if you don't have a room or space in your house specifically dedicated to arts and crafts, you can make the most of what you do have. Pay attention to the times in which you feel particularly creative. What are the conditions? Do you work best alone or in a group? Do you prefer to work in silence or with music or television in the background? By learning the conditions in which your creative self thrives, you can make it easier for you to be creative when you need to the most.

* WIRE'S UNLIMITED POTENTIAL

Wire's versatility makes it a wonderful brainstorming tool. Instead of waiting for your muse, create your own inspirational starting points.

For example, use pliers or a pencil to create a coil shape with your wire. Then create something with it. For example, add beads and wrap it around a votive, candlestick or champagne glass. There is no "right" way to create something new. Experiment and feel your creative confidence grow.

tablecloth weights

Tablecloth weights are a wonderfully practical project, perfect for picnics and outdoor dining. They are excellent hostess gifts at summertime parties. They also make charming pendants when one is strung from a necklace. This wire project is a great way to get the feel of working with wire and beads.

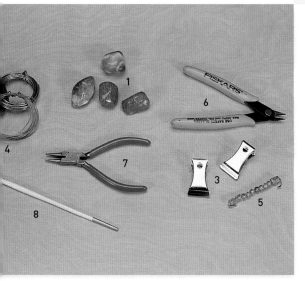

◄ **MATERIALS**

1 four polished, tumbled stones, approximately 1½" x 1" (3.5 x 2.5cm) each

2 18" (45.7cm) of 18-gauge plastic-coated craft wire

3 four metal clips (one for each weight)

4 24" (61cm) of 24-gauge plastic-coated craft wire

5 twenty-four glass beads

6 wire cutters

7 round-nose pliers

8 paintbrush or pencil

1 ▪ Begin a Spiral

Grasp the 18-gauge wire with your round-nose pliers and start a tight spiral with at least three revolutions. This will form the base of the tablecloth weight and will hold the stone in place. I used purple wire over a purple stone for a simple color palette.

2 ▪ Wrap the Wire Around the Stone

With your hands, wrap the wire around the stone, following the contours of the individual stone. It does not have to be tightly wrapped, but should be close enough to hold the stone in place.

3 ▪ Trim the Wire

Continue to wrap the wire around the stone until it covers the top. Cut the wire with wire cutters about 2½" (6.4cm) beyond the final loop at the top of the stone.

4 ▪ Attach the End to the Metal Clip

Wrap the excess wire through the hole in the metal clip, securing it firmly. You're done!

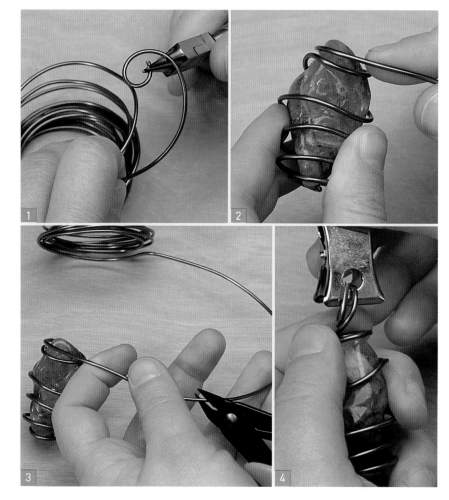

variation:
adding an extra twist

1 ▪ Make a Basic Tablecloth Weight

You can add glass beads to any tablecloth weight for more sparkle. Begin by making a tablecloth weight just like the first one. Choose whatever color of wire and stone you like best. In this variation, I chose 18-gauge copper-colored wire because I liked the way it contrasted with the green stone.

2 ▪ Coil the Wire Around a Brush Handle

To create a beaded coil, start by wrapping a length of 24-gauge wire around a narrow brush handle, pencil or other long, narrow object. I used about 24" (61cm) of wire for this stone. The length of wire you need may vary depending on the size and number of beads used as well as the overall size of the stone.

3 ▪ Add Beads as You Coil the Wire

Wrap a few coils around the brush handle, add a bead or two, then continue to wrap the wire. Continue to add beads and wrap the wire until you get to the end of the wire. Slide the coil of wire and beads off the brush handle.

4 ▪ Attach the Top of the Coil

Secure the first coils by wrapping them around the top of the stone with a pair of round- or needle-nose pliers.

5 ▪ Attach the Bottom of the Coil

Wrap the rest of the coil of wire and beads around the stone, tucking the beaded coil into the wire around the stone about every inch (2.5cm) to hold it in place. Use pliers to secure the end of the beaded wire at the bottom of the stone.

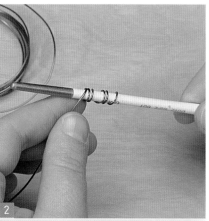

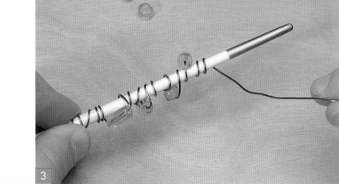

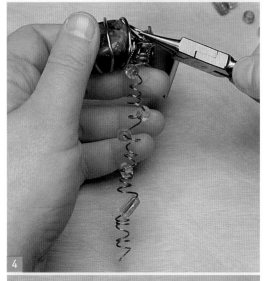

METAL & WIRE CRAFTS (**PROJECT TWO**)

aged-copper book

Combine bookmaking, rubber stamping and copper embossing metal to create this strikingly original project! This is an interesting project because we are working with liver of sulfur and petroleum jelly to create an instant antiqued effect. This is also an excellent project for learning basic embossing techniques on metal.

MATERIALS ➤

1. sheet of lightweight copper embossing foil

2. wax palette or wax paper

3. petroleum jelly

4. rubber stamp (All Night Media, Inc.: Swirl Pattern)

5. two cups of water in a plastic tub or bowl

6. liver of sulfur (potassium sulfide, sulfurated potash)

7. art fibers, yarn or narrow ribbon

8. parchment-colored paper cut to 3¼" x 26" (8.3 x 66cm)

9. assorted ¼" (6mm) beads

10. scissors

11. embossing stylus

[not shown]

12. rubber gloves

13. isopropyl alcohol

14. paper towels

15. glue stick

16. two squares of acid-free binder's board cut to 3½" x 3½" (9 x 9cm)

[optional]

17. white cardstock

1 ▪ Cut and Clean the Metal Foil

Because you will need a completely clean, oil-free surface for antiquing, put on gloves before you touch the metal up until the antiquing is done. Cut off a 5" x 9" (12.7 x 23cm) piece of copper metal with scissors. Next, moisten a paper towel with isopropyl alcohol and wipe down the entire surface to remove any dirt and oil. The cleaner the surface, the better the impression you will get with your stamp.

2 ▪ Spread Petroleum Jelly Onto The Palette

Spread a generous layer of petroleum jelly onto a wax palette or wax paper. There should be enough jelly on the surface so that the stamp will pick it up, but not so much that the jelly will get inside the crevices of the stamp and distort the stamped image.

3 ▪ Stamp the Pattern Onto the Metal

Place your stamp down onto the petroleum jelly the same way you would if you were using ink. Begin stamping the pattern on the metal. Carefully place the stamp down, press firmly and then lift directly up to remove.

tip Because the jelly is slick, be careful not to slide the stamp and distort the pattern. Don't worry if there is some overlap. With the swirling design, it does not need to be perfect.

4 ▪ Mix the Antiquing Solution

In a well-ventilated area, create an antiquing solution by mixing the liver of sulfur with water according to the directions on the bottle. I poured two capfuls of liver of sulfur to two cups of warm water in a plastic bowl.

NOTE: You should label this bowl afterwards, "For Craft Use Only." Do not use it for food.

5 ▪ Dip the Metal in the Solution

With your hands still covered by gloves, dip the metal sheet into the solution. Keep the metal in the solution until it attains the color you desire.

tip You may wish to cover your table with towels or plastic so that the solution does not drip and cause any harm.

6 ▪ Set the Sheet Aside to Dry

When you are happy with the color of the metal, take the sheet out of the solution and place it on a stack of paper towels. Allow it to air dry.

tip Dispose of the liver of sulfur solution by putting it on your outdoor plants. You can also mix it with baking soda until the fizzing stops, then add sawdust and put it out in the sun to dry and neutralize. At that point, you can bundle it into newspaper and throw it away.

7 ▪ Buff the Patterned Surface

When the metal is completely dry, use a paper towel or soft cloth to buff the metal. In some areas, the oxidization will flake off, so be sure to do this over a paper towel. The petroleum jelly will seal the newly oxidized areas and give the metal a soft sheen.

8 ▪ Emboss the Front of the Sheet

With a small metal stylus, trace around the edges of the stamp design on the front of the metal. You may want to do this in small sections as the pressure required can give your hands a workout! Continue until the entire design has been traced.

9 ▪ Emboss the Back of the Pattern

Turn the sheet over. You will see that the stylus created an overall pattern on the back of the metal. With your stylus, emboss a line on either side of the first tracing line. This will create much greater dimension on the cover side.

10 ▪ Cut the Metal in Half for Two Covers

See the subtle difference? The left portion of the metal has been embossed on both sides. The right has been embossed only on the front. Once you are done embossing both sides, cut the sheet in half with scissors to create two 5" x 4½" (12.7 x 11.5cm) sheets.

11 ▪ Glue the Covers to the Boards

Measure and cut two pieces of binder's board or other stiff cardboard to a 3½" (9cm) square. Apply adhesive to one side of the cardboard with a glue stick and press it onto the center of the back of the metal sheet. Repeat for the back cover.

tip If you live in an area that is very dry, glue sticks may not hold indefinitely. If this is a concern for you, use Perfect Paper Adhesive or other acid-free glue.

12 ▪ Cut Out the Flaps

With scissors, create flaps on both covers by cutting off notches on all four corners as shown in the photo.

tip Save the leftover scraps of embossed metal to use in a collage or other craft project.

13 ▪ Fold Down the Flaps

Fold each edge over onto the back of the cardboard. Because metal holds its form, you do not need to apply glue. However, if the piece is going to be handled often or you are concerned about it coming apart, you can apply glue to each edge before folding.

14 ▪ Attach the Fibers for Closing the Book

Glue two 21" (53.3cm) strands of art fiber to each side of one cover. This will become the back cover of the book, so choose which cover you like the best (in terms of the overall design) before gluing the strands in place. If you do not have art fibers, you can use ribbon, yarn or embroidery floss instead.

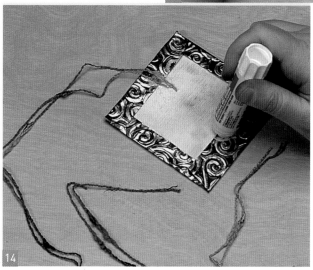

15 ▪ Fold and Glue in the Accordion Pages

Fold the 3¼" x 26" (8.3 x 66cm) strip of parchment paper into an accordion fold with eight panels. Refer to chapter five for detailed instructions on creating accordion books. Apply adhesive to each end of the accordion panel with a glue stick. Press the glued ends in place against the inside of each book cover. Allow it to dry well.

16 ▪ Add Beads to Embellish

The art fibers attached to the back cover will wrap around the book several times. For a finishing touch, tie beads to the end of the fibers.

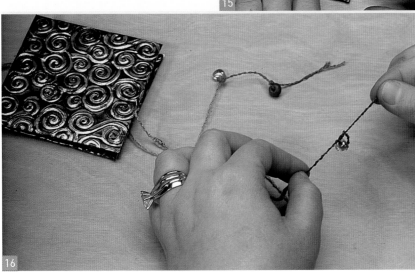

✳ places to find more inspiration

✳ *Several new books* feature projects that use craft-friendly wires and metals. Two titles you might like to try are Home and Garden Metalcrafts by Jana Ewy (North Light Books) and New Metalfoil Crafts by Barbara Matthiessen (Rockport Books).

✳ *Kathy Peterson* is a wire artist and author of several videos on wire crafts. Visit her Web site at www.kathy-peterson.com.

✳ *A good British Web site* for wire crafts is www.wire-magic.co.uk.

More Ways to Use Metal and Wire

- MAKE AN EMBOSSED gift box or create individual embossed elements to be cut out and pasted onto greeting cards.

- USE COLORED aluminum embossing metal to create ornaments. Cut out basic shapes and use an embossing tool to decorate.

- USE WIRE AND METAL to create a luminary. Cut out four panels and use a hole punch to create a design around the edges. Then "sew" the pieces together with contrasting wire.

- PRACTICE MAKING interesting jewelry pieces with different gauge wire.

floral topiaries
a time to blossom

lower arranging is a wonderful way to liberate your creativity. Flowers are beauty incarnate, so you simply can't go wrong practicing this craft! When arranging flowers, trust that when you aim to please your own eye, you'll naturally develop a personal sense of design. Look at arrangements in stores or magazines as a starting point, then substitute your favorite flowers to make your own creative statement!

CREATIVITY SESSION: *Death by Comparison*

[CREATIVE BLOCK]

Whenever I take a class or make a project from a book, I compare my work to the teacher's or the picture in the book and it never looks as good. I get discouraged because my work never measures up.

THERE IS NO COMPARISON

One of the easiest ways to burst your creative bubble is to compare your work to someone else's. What you are comparing is what you imagine their work process to be to the reality of your own life. That is like comparing a TV sitcom marriage to a real relationship.

When we compare ourselves (or our work) to other people, we create our own insecurity because our imaginings about what other people do are full of assumptions. We tend to assume that other people's creative work came easily to them. We assume that they didn't have any of the frustrations or challenges we have had to get the project completed. We also tend to expect ourselves to perform at the same skill level as the other person, whether that is possible or not.

These assumptions usually cast us in the "lesser" role and, to some extent, lessen the value of the work undertaken by the person to which we are comparing ourselves. If you assume that other artists' work comes to them with complete ease, you do not recognize the years of practice, learning and work they put into their craft. You do neither yourself, nor the person to which you compare yourself, credit when you compare.

CELEBRATE THE DIFFERENCES

When it comes to creativity, there is no "one way" that is right. That can be frustrating to the beginner. If there were only one "correct" way, arts and crafts would be a science! In order to grow creatively, you have to learn to embrace the value of the uniqueness of what you create. The differences in your work "compared" to another person's work is what makes what you do an art!

That is not to say that there are not benefits to looking at other artists' work. When you are taking a class, you want to look at what your teacher is doing to learn. This goes back to what we discussed in chapter four: give yourself permission to be a beginner and to learn. When you first begin your creative journey, your work may not be as good as your teacher's finished sample. At the same time, your teacher probably didn't create that sample in a classroom with distractions and limited supplies.

Use comparison as a tool to enhance your creative work by learning from it. Ask questions about why your work looks different. You may find that there are practical reasons for the differences: some paints are a different color when they dry or your teacher may have used slightly different products for the sample than those used in the class. Don't assume anything. Ask questions and learn. Comparison becomes a knife to your creative soul when you use it to denigrate your own work.

If you must compare, try comparing yourself today to yourself yesterday. In the words of Julia Cameron, "progress, not perfection" should be the goal.

floral topiaries: getting started

USE SILK FLOWERS FOR YOUR INITIAL VENTURES IN TOPIARIES. They come in as wide a variety as the real thing, plus their durability allows you to practice and experiment with multiple arrangements. Craft stores carry an amazing variety of silk flowers. Look for flowers with wire stems that can be bent into shape when you arrange them. If you are using more than one type of flower, choose shapes and colors that complement each other. In addition to flowers, you will also need a planter, floral foam to hold the stems in place, floral tape, wire, wire cutters, white glue, moss and any materials needed to decorate your planter.

There are several types of floral foam available. For silk floral arrangements you can use basic Styrofoam, although foam made for floral arrangements usually works better. Choose the foam best suited to your type of arrangement. If you aren't sure what to buy, read the packaging to find out the foam's purpose or ask the store employees.

As you gain experience and confidence, you may consider using real flowers. Arranging specimens from your very own garden brings even greater creative satisfaction!

confidence builders

* WHAT IS MISSING?

When you are not reaching your potential or are not on track, you may focus your attention on others who are where you would like to be. Jealousy is your mind's way of showing you what you are missing and where you would really like to be. This same emotion, however, can be horribly destructive. Envy can make you hateful. It can burn within you, making the person you envy a horrible villain in your mind. It can make you believe that when someone else does or owns something you want, they are keeping you from having it. How you use this emotion is your choice.

Think about the times in your life when that niggling feeling comes up for you. It is important to understand that jealousy may hit you even if it is not something that you have a desire to do. For example, a friend may get their first book published and you may feel that stirring even though you have no desire to write. If you pay attention to your feelings, you may see a pattern emerge. While you may not want to write, your longing to communicate through your painting or collage may be coming through.

Most of us are uncomfortable with jealousy. Feeling jealous does not mean that you would take something away from someone else. It can be a positive emotion if you channel it into learning about what you want.

hydrangea topiary

Loose, long-stemmed silk flowers can be gathered together to create an elegant topiary. The beauty of this project comes from decorating a planter and choosing ribbons that complement the color of your flowers. The gold in the container ties in well with the golden green of the hydrangea leaves.

MATERIALS

1 metal planter

2 thick white craft glue (Aleene's Tacky Glue)

3 floral foam

4 one bouquet of purple silk hydrangeas

5 floral tape

6 18" (45.7cm) of purple 18-gauge plastic-coated craft wire

7 purple acrylic paint (FolkArt purple)

8 Spanish moss

9 48" (122cm) of white wire-edge ribbon

10 wire cutters

11 no. 20 flat brush

12 palette paper

13 water bin

14 scissors

[not shown]

15 metal primer

16 knife

1 ▪ Add Glue to the Planter

Pour a swirl of thick white craft glue into the bottom of the metal planter.

2 ▪ Add the Floral Foam

Cut the floral foam with a knife into sections and wedge it firmly into the planter. If the foam is stacked, be sure to apply glue between each layer. If you prefer, you can use glue made specifically for foam.

3 ▪ Cut Flowers From the Bouquet

With wire cutters, cut each flower stem off the stalk. Cut the lower leaves off the stems.

4 ▪ Cut Off the Thorns

If there are thorns, use wire cutters to trim these off as well. The idea is to get the stems to bundle as closely together as possible.

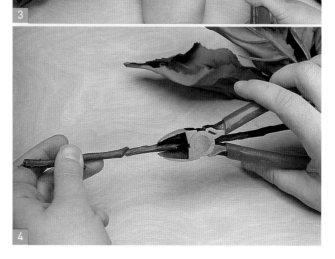

5 ▪ Bundle the Stems Together

Bundle the stems together and rearrange the leaves so that they are positioned around the bottoms of the flowers.

6 ▪ Wrap the Stems With Floral Tape

Wrap the stems with floral tape. Floral tape is a sticky form of crepe paper. It will stretch and tear in the same way. Pull it tight as you wind it around the stems to hold them together.

7 ▪ Wrap the Wire Around the Stems

Loosely wind about 18" (45.7cm) of purple 18-gauge wire around the stems. This step provides additional color to the stems and visually ties the metal planter to the flowers. Cut any leftover wire with wire cutters and tuck the loose end between the stems at the bottom of the bundle.

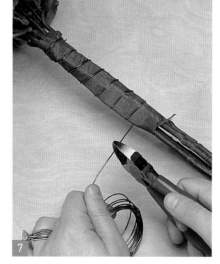

✳ practical magic

Floral design is a practical and personal form of creative expression. Since each flower is unique and there are many styles of planters, the same techniques can create very different results. Fresh flowers are widely available, but silk flowers are also an excellent choice because of their durability. Give yourself the time to try many different arrangements, bringing a bit of creative magic into your home and life.

8 ▪ Paint the Planter

With a no. 20 flat brush, paint the metal planter purple if it doesn't match the floral design. It will likely require more than one coat for complete coverage. If the planter will get a lot of use, prime the container first with a metal primer to ensure that the paint won't peel or scratch off.

9 ▪ Plant the Flowers

When the paint is dry, push the flowers firmly into the floral foam base. The flowers should be stable. If not, add additional foam around the base or shorten the stems.

10 ▪ Add Glue for the Moss

Apply thick white craft glue to the base of the foam. Squeeze some additional glue around the base of the stems to further hold them in place.

✳ be observant

Nurture your creativity by becoming more observant. Beauty surrounds you in a multitude of ways. Sometimes you have to look for it, not because it is such a small part of our lives but because we are overwhelmed with what surrounds us and we become numb to it. Observe the way light filters through your cat's fur, the sound of your child splashing in the tub, the taste of ice cream on your tongue. Inspiration need not be found in the exotic. Look to the details of your life and see what you have been missing.

11 ▪ Add the Moss

Add Spanish moss to cover the foam and the base of the stems. Next, tie the center of a 48" (122cm) length of wire-edge ribbon at the base of the flower stems.

12 ▪ Weave the Ribbon

Crisscross the ribbon upward around the stems and tie a knot at the top.

13 ▪ Tie a Bow

To finish your topiary, tie a bow and use your fingers to curl the ribbon ends. If the ribbon is frayed or too long, trim the ends with scissors.

✳ exercise: creative mentors

Success is like a path. Each person who goes down it tramples the foliage a bit more, making it easier for the next person who comes along. You can have many reactions to the success of others. You can be grateful for their success as pioneers and good examples of how hard work can pay off. You can become angry at the injustice of their success when you are still struggling. You can celebrate their success because those niggling jealous thoughts spur you to work harder.

Make a list of people who are doing the kinds of things you would like to do. Do a bit of research to learn about their lives. What can you learn from them? What mistakes did they make that you can avoid?

rose topiary

The variegated colors of the roses in this topiary are cheerful and inviting. Yellow is an excellent neutral color for the pot, so you could create this design with virtually any color of flower. The wide variety of flowers available allow you to create many different effects even with the same basic design. This variation on the Hydrangea Topiary project is fun because it lets you practice using a simple topiary form.

MATERIALS →

1   4½" (11.4cm) terra cotta pot

2   four bunches of silk rosebuds in two shades of pink

3   4½" (11.4cm) diameter topiary form

4   no. 20 flat brush

5   no. 12 flat brush

6   thick white craft glue (Aleene's Tacky Glue)

7   yellow, green and pink acrylic paints (Folk Art Sunflower, Clover and Spring Rose)

8   wire cutters

9   Spanish moss

10   water basin

11   wax palette or plate

[not shown]

12   no. 2 liner brush

[optional]

13   nail file or fine sandpaper

14   sponge

15   no. 6 filbert brush

1 ▪ Clean the Pot

Wash down a 4½" (11.4cm) terra cotta pot with a damp sponge. Allow it to dry. If the pot is rough, use a nail file or sandpaper to smooth those areas.

2 ▪ Paint the Pot Yellow

With a no. 20 flat brush, paint the pot with Sunflower. It will take at least two coats to fully cover it. Let each coat dry well before continuing.

3 ▪ Cut the Rosebuds Off the Bunch

While your pot is drying, use wire cutters to cut each rosebud off the stem about ¼" (.6cm) below the calyx.

4 ▪ Poke Holes for the Rose Stems

If your topiary form is dense and hard, create an indentation in the topiary form with scissor blades before affixing each flower firmly into the form. Place the indentations close enough together so that none of the form shows between the roses. You can skip this step with softer topiary forms.

5 ▪ Glue in Each Rosebud

Add the rosebuds one by one. After you poke each hole, put a dot of thick white craft glue into each indentation to hold the rose in place.

6 ▪ Cover the Form With Rosebuds

Attach the rosebuds in a random pattern, varying the colors against one another until you have covered the entire form. Allow the glue to dry well.

7 ▪ Decorate the Rim

Paint a wavy wreath around the rim of the pot using a liner brush and Clover thinned with water. Allow the lines to intersect. Vary the thickness of the lines as you paint.

tip If you wish, go back to page 30 for a demonstration on how to paint these fine, wavy lines and practice on paper before you paint on your pot.

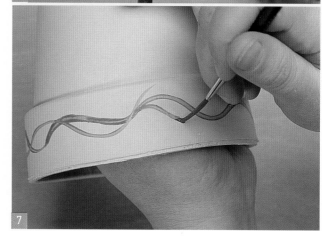

8 ▪ Load the Brush

The leaves on the pot can be painted with
a no. 6 filbert brush. A filbert is a specialty
brush shaped like a flat brush with
rounded edges. Load the filbert by dipping
it into the paint about three-quarters up
the bristles.

tip If you don't have a filbert, a no. 8 flat
brush will do.

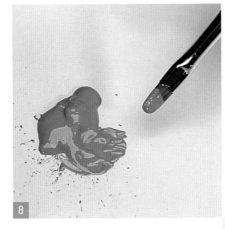

9 ▪ Begin the Leaf Stroke

This leaf is called a one-stroke leaf because
you create it with a single stroke of the
brush. With your hand braced, push the
brush down to the flat so that the sides of
the bristles are on your surface. The splay
of the bristles will create the rounded
edge of the leaf.

10 ▪ Finish the Leaf

Pull your brush in the direction you want
your leaf. As you lift the downward pressure, turn the brush one-quarter turn. End
the stroke with the bristles back up on the
chisel edge (the very tips of the bristles).

11 ▪ Paint Leaves Around the Rim of the Pot

Paint a variety of leaves around the rim of the pot over the painted vines. Be sure to vary the size and direction of the leaves around the pot.

12 ▪ Load the Handle With Paint

Dip the handle of one of the brushes into a puddle of Spring Rose.

13 ▪ Decorate the Pot With Dots

Place dots in a random pattern around the pot. Set the pot aside to dry.

14 ▪ Glue the Topiary Into The Pot

Once your pot is dry, apply glue to the base of the topiary form and insert it into the pot.

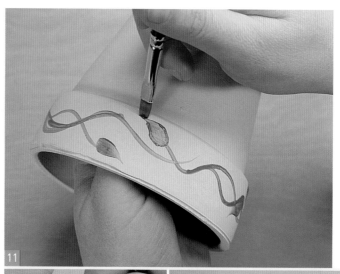

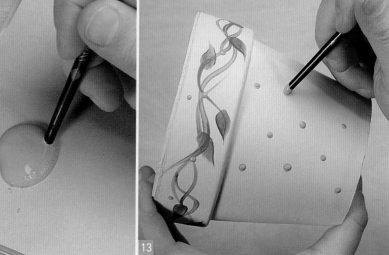

15 ▪ Add Spanish Moss

Squeeze more glue on top of the base and add Spanish moss around the base of the pot. If the moss overhangs the pot, trim it with scissors once the glue has dried.

✳ resources for more inspiration

✳ *Good step-by-step project books* can take the guesswork out of making a beautiful arrangement. Try Fabulous Silk Florals for the Home *by Cele Kahle (North Light Books) or* Wreaths for Every Season *by June Apel (North Light Books).*

✳ *Free floral project guides* can be found at *www.i-craft.com/general/#floral.*

✳ *Check out this floral design instruction Web site, which includes information on working with different kinds of flowers, arranging basics and more: www.save-on-crafts.com/inonflordesa.html.*

✳ *Find tips* for basic floral design at the DIY Network:*www.diynet.com/DIY/article/0,2058,241,00.html.*

More Ways to Use Silk Flowers

• CUT ROSEBUDS, such as those used in the Rose Topiary, can be used in designs for shadow boxes, on lampshades, pillows and more.

• LONG-STEMMED, oblong-shaped flowers such as roses and tulips work well for the long-stemmed topiary design. The smaller the flower, the more flowers you will need to create the full head of the topiary. Fuller flowers, such as hydrangeas and peonies, also work well in bunches.

• BECAUSE OF THE WIDE VARIETY of flowers available, you can create many variations using the same basic design elements. Imagine the rose topiary created with daisies, for example.

variation

[EACH TOPIARY IS UNIQUE] This variation shows how just a little change can make a difference in the way a project will turn out. This topiary uses half- and fully-opened rosebuds that are all the same shade of pink. The roses were applied in the same manner as the variegated rose design. Notice how the use of leaves interspersed with the flowers provides contrast and visual interest.

mosaics
going to pieces

mosaic is like a puzzle with a million different solutions—and every one of them has its own beauty and charm. A risk-free art, mosaic lets you perfect your design before gluing it into place. It's easy to experiment with colors and patterns until you find a look you like. Make a few mosaics and you'll be amazed at how your creative efforts can transform common items into artful decorations.

CREATIVITY SESSION: Letting Go of Expectations

[CREATIVE BLOCK]

I can't get started because I know I'll never be able to create something like I picture it in my mind.

USE MORE THAN YOUR IMAGINATION

Part of expanding your creativity is the trial and error that results in the finished product. Contrary to what you may believe, few artists imagine a project in exact detail before creating it. Indeed, many artists create dozens of sketches and prototypes before they start to work.

This fear ties in to the "I'm not an artist unless I can…" fear. A couple of years ago, I was talking to an editor who had recently returned from a photo shoot with a well-known artist. She was shocked to learn that the artist worked from photographs. This artist was so talented, the editor assumed that she just imagined her subject and painted it. In reality, the artist had an entire library in her studio dedicated to photographs, books, sketches and other reference materials from which she worked.

MAKE A PLAN

Instead of postponing your creative journey because you aren't a camera, try developing a plan of action. Creativity is problem solving. The first step is to define the problem or issue. Do this in the form of a question. For example, "How can I draw a realistic-looking rose?"

Once you have a question in mind, brainstorm ideas. The key to brainstorming is to avoid analyzing the ideas until you have created a list. Here is the result of my brainstorm session for this question:

- Get a book on drawing flowers.
- Channel Michelangelo.
- Get a video on drawing so I can watch someone draw a rose.
- Find a local class on drawing still lifes.
- Gather some roses from the yard and practice drawing them.
- Talk to my neighbor's son who is good at drawing.
- Get a clip art book on roses and practice tracing the outline to learn the shape.
- Call my old high school art teacher and ask for private lessons.

As soon as you have a good list of ideas, you will need to look at them based upon the practicalities of your situation. While "gathering roses from the yard" is a good suggestion, it might not be practical if you don't have any rose bushes or they aren't blooming at present. Channeling Michelangelo is nice work if you can get it, but probably not likely. Prioritize the list by practicality and appeal.

Finally, choose one action and determine what it will take to make it happen. If you choose "get a video" or "get a book," you may have to go to a bookstore. If you already have a book, you may only need to gather your materials and get started. No matter what, do one thing today. If it doesn't work, go back to your brainstorming list. Keep trying until you find something that helps you learn and gives you confidence toward reaching your final goal.

mosaics: getting started

MOSAICS CAN BE MADE FROM JUST ABOUT ANYTHING. Old plates, tile, glass, pebbles and other small, hard objects will work just fine. Bring together patterns, colors and shapes that are visually appealing. Although it may be tempting to throw away blank, left-over pieces, save them. Most designs benefit from single color pieces combined with patterned pieces. When it comes to mosaics, nothing is wasted!

You can purchase prepackaged tiles, mosaic grout and adhesive made specifically for tiling or mosaic work at most craft or home improvement stores. To break large tiles or old china plates into smaller pieces, you will also want a tile "nipper" or cutter. For safety's sake, always wear protective gloves and eyewear whenever you are cutting tile.

Mosaics can be applied to almost any smooth, hard surface. I find papier mâché ideal, but you can also use wood, glass or metal. Acrylic paint is also good to have on hand for coloring the grout or painting any trim to match the color of your tiles.

confidence builders

* MAKE A PAPER MOSAIC

If working with glass, china and tile seems a bit intimidating, start with paper. Simply paint a piece of wood or cardboard gray or white. This will imitate the "grout" portion of the mosaic.

Cut up a magazine ad, photocopied photograph or wrapping paper to create your "tiles." Play around with arranging these tiles on your surface until you come up with a pattern you like. You can add texture to your paper "tiles" with a dimensional sealer such as Diamond Glaze for a more realistic appearance.

Working with paper mosaics will help you gain confidence working on a layout before getting started in glass or tile.

* SERENDIPITY COLLAGE

In my studio, I use cardstock to protect my table when I paint small objects. Over time, these pages develop interesting patterns of inter-secting colors and shapes. Rather than just throw the paper away, I cut it up into squares and use them to create collage designs.

You can do this on your own by filling up a page with lines and squiggles using paint, markers, glitter and more. When it dries, put a 1" (2.5cm) square (or smaller) stencil over the top and look for the most interesting designs in that small space. As you move the stencil around the sheet, you will be surprised at the beautiful designs that emerge when you look at them out of the context of the full sheet. Trace and cut these squares, then paste them onto a complementary colored background for a fun, and serendipitous, art project.

mosaic trunk

New mosaic products make creating your own mosaics easy!
This charming papier mâché trunk project will teach you basic mosaic skills.

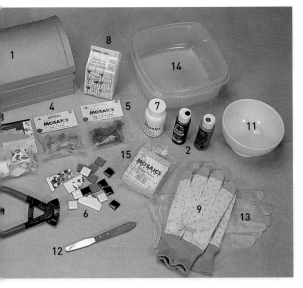

MATERIALS

1 6" x 9" x 5" (15.2 x 23 x 12.7cm) papier mâché trunk

2 medium blue and deep blue acrylic paint (FolkArt Sterling Blue and Thunder Blue)

3 blue and white vintage floral mosaic tiles (enough for fifty ½" to ¾" [1.3 to 2cm] pieces)

4 twenty-five royal blue ¾" (2cm) tile chips

5 twenty-five blue glass ¾" (2cm) tile chips

6 twenty-five to thirty white ¾" (2cm) tile chips

7 tile adhesive (or craft glue)

8 1 lb. (45g) tile grout

9 leather gloves

10 tile nippers

11 mixing bowl for grout

12 palette knife or spatula

13 rubber or latex gloves

14 basin of water

15 sponge

[not shown]

16 no. 20 flat brush

17 safety goggles

1 ▪ Paint the Box Trim

With a no. 20 flat brush, paint the trim around the box in Sterling Blue. There is no need to paint the box where the mosaic design will be placed.

2 ▪ Cut the Floral Tiles

Put on leather gloves to protect your hands and a pair of glasses or safety goggles to protect your eyes from splinters of tile and glass. Carefully break the vintage mosaic floral tiles into ¾" (2cm) pieces, roughly the same size as the solid blue square tiles. The pieces need to be small enough that they will not stick up on the curved lid of the box. The nippers will cut along the line of the blade and beyond, following the same line. Position the blade carefully to maximize the pattern.

3 ▪ Apply the Tile Adhesive

With a no. 20 flat brush, apply adhesive to the surface where the tile will be placed, and then apply adhesive to the back of the tile before placing each tile on the box. With a vertical or curved surface, it is difficult to lay out the design in advance. Simply vary the tile and glass chips in color and size next to one another as you go.

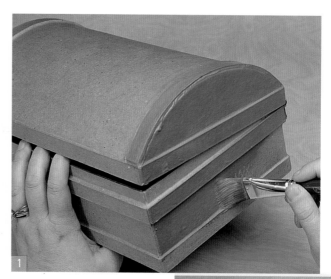

✳ creative excursion

Creating mosaics is much more personal when you can use your own "finds" in your designs. Visit garage and tag sales, thrift shops and second-hand stores for inexpensive china and tile.

4 ▪ Mix the Grout

Pour ½ lb. (22g) of tile grout mix into a
bowl, then add a bit of water according to
the directions on the package. Generally,
the mix is about three parts grout to one
part water. Add about a dime-size dollop of
Thunder Blue into the grout mixture and
stir. Add paint until the color is slightly
darker than the color of the box. Keep in
mind that the grout will get lighter while
it dries.

5 ▪ Check the Color and Consistency

The texture of the grout should be approximately that of thick oatmeal. It should not
be soupy or wet. If needed, keep adding
more paint until you like the color. The
grout will dry slightly lighter than it
appears when wet.

6 ▪ Apply the Grout to the Box

Cover your hands with rubber or latex
gloves and begin applying the grout to the
box. I like to use my hands so that I can
push the grout between the tiles and work
it into place. Because the cut tile will be
uneven, you will need to push the grout
carefully in between and under the tiles
where the box curves.

7 ▪ Clean Up the Rough Edges

You can use a spatula or palette knife
along the edges of the box to get an even
surface. If there is a lot of grout over and
around the tile, wipe the pieces gently
with a wet sponge until the grout is even.

8 ▪ Rub the Excess Grout Off the Tiles

When the grout is in place, use your finger to rub off the grout residue from each mosaic piece. This helps ensure that you haven't buried a piece under the grout accidentally. Let the grout dry thoroughly.

tip Once the grout dries, it is much harder to break if you want to uncover a tile, so be sure the grout is smoothed out and the tiles are fairly clean before it dries.

9 ▪ Wipe the Tiles Clean

After allowing the grout to dry at least an hour, wipe the tops of each mosaic piece with a clean sponge and water. Have a bowl or water basin handy because you will want to rinse the sponge several times during the process.

10 ▪ Tile the Sides and Touch Up With Paint

Repeat the process for applying the tiles along the sides of the box. Let each side dry thoroughly before turning the box. Touch up the blue paint on the edges of the box where the grout caused discoloration.

china mosaic frame

This mosaic is both practical and inexpensive. By recycling plates found at garage sales or thrift shops, this china cost only pennies! This is a great way to recycle your own china if it gets broken accidentally. A frame or clock in the kitchen that "happens" to match your china is a wonderful accessory.

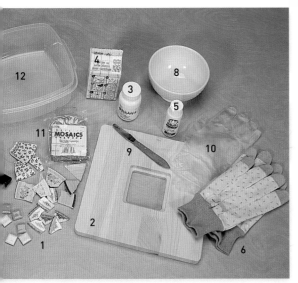

▼ MATERIALS

1 two 10" (25.4cm) diameter dinner plates, broken into fragments

2 10" x 10" (25.4 x 25.4cm) wooden frame

3 tile adhesive

4 1 lb. (45g) of mosaic tile grout

5 light green acrylic paint (FolkArt Hauser Green Light)

6 leather gloves

7 tile nippers

8 mixing bowl for grout

9 palette knife or spatula

10 plastic or rubber gloves

11 sponge

12 basin of water

[not shown]

13 twenty ¾" (2cm) royal blue mosaic tile chips

14 safety goggles

15 no. 20 flat brush

1 ▪ Lay Out Your Design

With a flat surface, you can lay out your design in advance. In this case, I have taken two 10" (25.4cm) plates found at a garage sale and reassembled them to the shape of a single plate, mixing and matching the designs. Dark blue square tiles anchor the edges and rim of the frame.

2 ▪ Apply Adhesive to the Frame

Leaving each piece in place, lift them one at a time and apply a generous dab of adhesive to the surface.

3 ▪ Apply Adhesive to the Tiles

Apply adhesive to the back of the tile or china piece and then press into place. Applying adhesive to both the wood and the tile will ensure that the tile adheres completely to the wood. Continue until all the pieces are glued and the adhesive is dry.

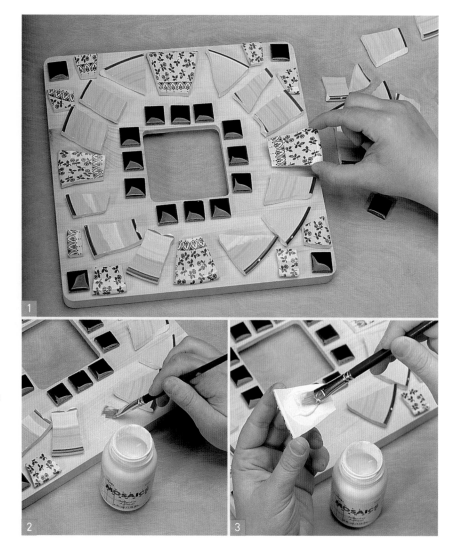

Using Tile Nippers • Tile nippers will cut along and beyond the line of the nipper blade. Since plates are curved, it can be a challenge to cut around the painted design on the plate. Create large cuts first, breaking the plate into manageable pieces along sections that are not decorated, then begin cutting out individual sections or designs in small sections.

If your tile or plate has an overall pattern with no specific element you want to showcase, you can place it between several layers of newspaper and use a rubber mallet or hammer to break it.

4 ▪ Prepare the Grout

Pour ½ lb. (22g) of grout mix into a clean bowl. Add water a small amount at a time.

tip Generally, the mix is three parts grout to one part water, but humidity and weather conditions may affect this. Follow the directions for the product you choose.

5 ▪ Check the Consistency

Stir the grout and water mixture until it is approximately the consistency of oatmeal. The grout should not be soupy or wet. It should hold together in a lump or ball without crumbling.

6 ▪ Apply the Grout

With your hands covered with plastic or rubber gloves, apply the grout over the tiled surface a section at a time. Use your fingers to press the grout in between the tiles and under the edge of the china pieces.

7 ▪ Work the Grout Between the Tiles

Continue to add grout to the tiled surface. When you use china in your mosaic, the pieces will not glue flush to the surface, so you will have to work the grout under any small gaps between the tiles and the surface. Then work more grout in between the pieces so there are no bubbles.

8 ▪ Smooth Any Rough Edges

Make sure that the edges where the grout meets the frame are smooth and rounded. Try to avoid creating any rough edges that might cut or catch your hands when you handle the frame after the grout dries.

9 ▪ Rub Excess Grout From The Tiles

When the grout is in place, use your finger to rub off the grout residue from each mosaic piece. This helps you make sure you haven't buried a piece under the grout accidentally. Let the grout dry thoroughly.

10 ▪ Wipe the Tiles Clean

After allowing the grout to dry at least an hour, clean the tops of each mosaic piece with a clean sponge and water. Have a bowl or water basin handy because you will want to rinse the sponge several times during the process.

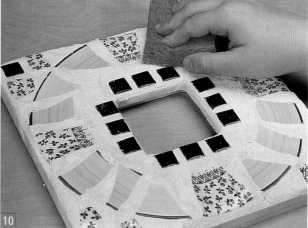

11 ▪ Paint the Wood Trim

With a no. 20 flat brush, paint the exposed wood on the sides and center of the frame with a matching color paint. Because of the bright green color in the plates, I used Hauser Green Light on this frame.

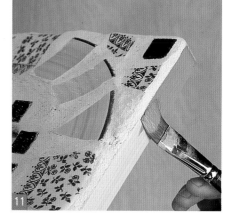

12 ▪ Finish Painting the Frame

Be sure to paint the back of your wooden frame so that the piece looks finished should anyone see it from the back.

✳ additional inspiration from the muses

✳ *There are dozens of good books that will teach you how to decorate with mosaics. For a bit of variety, look for* Easy Mosaics for Your Home and Garden *by Sarah Donnelly (North Light) and* Pebble Mosaics *by Ann Firth (David & Charles). For advice on colors and patterns, try* The Mosaic Idea Book *by Rosalind Wates (North Light Books).*

✳ *For sheer inspiration, read* Mosaics: Inspiration and Original Projects for Interiors and Exteriors *by Kaffe Fassett and Candace Bahouth (Taunton Press). Fassett's exuberant and colorful mosaics will give you a great idea of how far mosaic arts can go with a big imagination.*

✳ *On the Internet, check out the Society of American Mosaic Artists at www.americanmosaics.org. Artist Cole Sonafrank provides a large list of links to other mosaic-related artists, suppliers and informational Web sites at www.elvesofester. com/MosaicLinks.html. Mosaic Matters is a British online magazine for "all things mosaic." Visit it at www.users. dircon.co.uk/~asm.*

variation

[TRY DIFFERENT COLORS]

This photo shows another variation of the same design using two different plates with a pink and yellow design. Using the same techniques with different colors can produce a very different look.

More Ways to Play with Mosaics

Mosaics are addictive! Here is a list of creative ideas I've used.

● **DECORATE YOUR GARDEN** with a brightly colored mosaic birdbath, stepping-stones or plant pots.

● **LOOK FOR INTERESTING** surfaces for your mosaics at a local craft or hobby store. These might include vases, wooden boxes, birdhouses or switch plates.

● **RECYCLE** an old side table by covering it with a new mosaic top.

● **EXPERIMENT** with your designs by adding large glass beads, seashells, coins or colorful pebbles to your mosaic.

● **PRACTICE ARRANGING** your colored tiles to form fun shapes and patterns in your mosaics. Try laying the pattern of a single leaf or piece of fruit in the center of a trivet or large bowl. Part of the fun comes from finding the right mosaic pieces to fit in the shape.

a final word
of encouragement

y hope is that this book has inspired you to embark on your own creative journey. As you continue, remember that inside of you are strength, power and more creative ideas than you can ever use in one lifetime. Creativity is a basic problem-solving skill we all possess. Learn to be a kind to yourself, take the risk of being a beginner, learn something new. Creative confidence comes with experience, practice and time.

Even with all the creative power that is within you, Michelangelo will likely not spring out of you whole. You are going to begin a bit creaky and rusty, and will need some practice.

As you practice your crafts and proceed on your creative journey, expect learning, not perfection. Be realistic with your expectations. If you are working at a full-time job, have kids at home or have other major responsibilities, you will have less time to devote to your creative journey than you would probably like. That does not mean it isn't worth every moment you can spare. It does mean that you need to be even kinder to yourself when you are frustrated with your progress.

As you try new crafts, unleash your limitless creative powers upon every new project you begin. Release yourself from what other people have told you and ask yourself what you really believe. Trust the voice inside you.

Anne Lamott wrote that most people live their lives like the professor on Gilligan's Island. "They make generators out of palm fronds, and vaccinations from algae, but they never quite get around to fixing the hole in the boat so they can go home." Sound familiar?

When we started on this journey together, we talked about evaluating your fears, looking at your self-esteem, dealing with criticism and learning to place a value on your own creativity. If you think about it, it takes a lot of creative energy to have distracted yourself so successfully from your creative voice. These distractions are the generators and vaccinations of your personal "Gilligan's Island." Now that you have freed your creativity you are ready to start the journey home.

resources
If you are fortunate enough to have a local craft store, please ask them about the supplies found in this book. Even if they don't currently carry the supplies, they may be willing to order them for you. Supporting local shops helps ensure the shops will be around when you need them.

general craft supplies

If you don't have a local shop, or the shop cannot order the supplies found in the book, the following list of retailers may help.

A.C. Moore: www.acmoore.com
Hobby Lobby: www.hobbylobby.com
JoAnn Fabrics & Crafts, JoAnn Etc.: www.joanns.com
Michaels: www.michaels.com
Pearl Paint: www.pearlpaint.com

Craft Canada: www.craftcanada.com
Arts & Crafts Canada: www.artsandcraftscanada.com

In the UK (telephone for a store near you):
Craft World: 07000 757070
Hobby Crafts: 0800 272387

craft tools

Fiskars Brands, Inc.
7811 W. Stewart Ave.
Wausau, WI 54401
(800) 950-0203
www.fiskars.com
Personal Paper Trimmer; Colonial Pattern Paper Edgers (Paris Montage Card, p. 17); Fiskars Craft Mat (Lock and Key Book, p. 57); hole punch (Heart-Shaped Gift Tag, p. 76; Starry Book, p. 70); wire cutters, round-nose pliers (Tablecloth Weights, p. 83; Rose Topiary, p. 100)

Speedball Art Products Company
2226 Speedball Rd.
Statesville, NC 28677
(800) 898-7224
www.speedballart.com
Pop-In Soft Rubber Brayer (Lock and Key Book, p. 57; Umbrella Book, p. 62)

craft adhesives

All Night Media
Plaid Enterprises, Inc.
3225 Westech Dr.
Norcross, GA 30092-3500
(800) 842-4197
www.plaidonline.com
All Night Media Pop Dots (Paris Montage Card, p. 17)

UHU America, Inc.
61 Nickerson Hill Rd.
Readfield, ME 04335-0122
(207) 685-3385
www.uhu.de/_uk/indexx.html
Uhu Glue Stic

Duncan Enterprises, Inc.
5673 E. Shields Ave.
Fresno, CA 93727
(800) 438-6226
www.duncan-enterprises.com
Aleene's Quick Dry Tacky Glue (Umbrella Book, p. 62; Hydrangea Topiary, p. 95; Rose Topiary, p. 100)

US Artquest, Inc.
7800 Ann Arbor Rd.
Grass Lake, MI 49240
(800) 200-7848
www.usartquest.com
Perfect Paper Adhesive Matte (China Album, p. 49)

Talas
368 Broadway
New York, NY 10012
(212) 219-0710
www.talas-nyc.com
PVA glue

rubber stamp supplies

Ranger Industries, Inc.
15 Park Road
Tinton Falls, NJ 07724
800-244-2211
www.rangerink.com/
Ranger Heatit Craft Tool; Adirondack Dye Ink Acid; Free Color It Embossing Pad; Ancient Gold; Embossing Powder ; Super Fine Detail Embossing Powder ; Clear Embossing Ink ; (Paris Montage Card, p. 17; Deco Geisha Card, p. 22; Lock and Key Book, p. 57)

PSX
360 Sutton Pl.
Santa Rosa, CA 95407
(800) 782-6748
www.psxdesign.com
New Lands stamp (Paris Montage Card, p.17);
Paris Montage stamp (Paris Montage Card, p. 17)

JudiKins
17803 S. Harvard Blvd.
Gardena, CA 90248
(310) 515-1115
www.judi-kins.com
Deco Geisha stamp (Deco Geisha Card, p. 22);
Keyhole stamp (Lock and Key Book, p. 57);
Warm Colors Decorative Tassels (Deco Geisha
Card, p. 22)

All Night Media
Plaid Enterprises, Inc.
3225 Westech Dr.
Norcross, GA 30092-3500
(800) 842-4197
www.plaidonline.com
Swirl Pattern stamp (Aged-Copper Book, p. 86)

Stampinks Unlimited
P.O. Box 97
Shortsville, NY 14548
www.stampinks.com
general stamps and stamping supplies

decorative painting supplies

Pébéo
P.O. Box 717
555 VT Route 78, Airport Rd.
Swanton, VT 05488
(819) 829-5012
www.pebeo.com
Pébéo Vitrea 160 Veil White Glass Paint; Pébéo
Vitrea 160 Gold Transparent Outliner (Fishbowl Glass
Vase, p. 38)

FolkArt Paints
Plaid Enterprises, Inc.
3225 Westech Dr.
Norcross, GA 30092-3500
(800) 842-4197
www.plaidonline.com
FolkArt Acrylic Paints; FolkArt Outdoor Matte
Sealer; FolkArt Satin Artist's Varnish (Whimsical
Painted Box, p. 32, Hydrangea Topiary, p. 95;
Mosaic Trunk, p. 109; China Mosaic Frame, p. 113)

Houston Art, Inc.
10770 Moss Ridge Rd.
Houston, TX 77043-1175
(800) 272-3804
www.houstonart.com
gray waxed painting palettes

Walnut Hollow Farm, Inc.
1409 State Rd. 23
Dodgeville, WI 35533-2112
(800) 950-5101
www.walnuthollow.com
Ballfoot Personal Box (Whimsical Painted Box, p. 32)

Daler-Rowney, USA
2 Corporate Dr.
Cranbury, NJ 08512-9584
(609) 655-5252
www.daler-rowney.com
Robert Simmons Sapphire Series Brushes: liner
brushes (S51 series), filbert brushes (S67 series),
round brushes (S85 series), flat brushes (S60
series); water bins

Daler-Rowney, Ltd. UK
12 Percy St.
London W1A 2BP
England
071 636 8241

George Weil Fibrecrafts
Old Portsmouth Road
Peasmarsh
Guildford, Surrey, GU3 1L
0 (44) 1483 565800
www.georgeweil.co.uk
glass paint

Scumble Goosie
Lewiston Mill
Toadsmoor Road
Stroud, Gloucestershire GL5 2TB
01453-731305
www.scumble-goosie.co.uk
découpage papers

collage & découpage supplies

The McCall Pattern Company
P.O. Box 3100
Manhattan, KS 66505-3100
(800) 255-2762 ext 485
www.wallies.com
Wallies Dragonflies (Dragonfly Journal, p. 46)

US Artquest, Inc.
7800 Ann Arbor Rd.
Grass Lake, MI 49240
(800) 200-7848
www.usartquest.com
Perfect Paper Adhesive Matte (China Album, p. 49)

Northern Lights Designs
5221 Erskine Way S.W.
Seattle, WA 98136
(206) 353-2519
www.northernlightsdesigns.com
Artistic Collage Series Sheets: The Fragile Past,
No. 1 (China Album, p. 49); Travel Adventures, No.
1 (Travel Album, p. 45)

EK Success
P.O. Box 1141
Clifton, NJ 07014-1141
(800) 524-1349
www.eksuccess.com
Zig Opaque Writer 6mm Chisel Tip, Anniversary
Ivory; (Dragonfly Journal, p. 46; China Album, p. 49)

Scumble Goosie
Lewiston Mill
Toadsmoor Road
Stroud, Gloucestershire GL5 2TB
01453-731305
www.scumble-goosie.co.uk
découpage papers

ADDITIONAL COLLAGE SUPPLIERS ONLINE

Rubber Baby Buggy Bumpers:
www.rubberbaby.com
Artistic Enhancements:
www.artisticenhancements.com
In Your Dreams: www.geocities.com/
inyourdreamsonline/company.html
Mantofev: www.mantofev.com/home.html
Era Graphics:
www.eragraphics.com/silverpennies.html

bookmaking & paper supplies

theCardLadies
c/o Tamra Davis
9609 Farmridge Ln.
Matthews, NC 28105
www.thecardladies.com
theCardLadies Art Fibers (Lock and Key Book, p. 57;
Starry Book, p. 69; Heart-Shaped Gift Tag, p. 76)

Hero Arts
1343 Powell St.
Emeryville, CA 94608
(800) 222-HERO
www.heroarts.com
Crepe Yuzen paper (Deco Geisha Card, p. 22)

Paper Reflections
DMD Industries, Inc.
2300 S. Old Missouri Rd.
Springdale, AR 72764
(800) 805-9890
www.dmdind.com
green and cream cardstock (Deco Geisha Card, p.
22); black handmade paper (Paris Montage Card,
p. 17); red paper with gold threads (Paris Montage
Card, p. 17); spiral-bound memory books (Dragonfly Journal, p. 46; China Album, p. 49)

Flax Art & Design, Inc. (The Paper Catalog)
1699 Market St.
San Francisco, CA 94103
(800) 343-3529
www.flaxart.com
black and cream patterned paper (Lock and Key Book,
p. 57); handmade papers (Umbrella Book, p. 62)

Paper Habitat: www.paperhabitat.com

Volcano Book Arts:
www.volcanobookarts.com

Papers by Catherine:
www.papersbycatherine.com

papermaking supplies

Yasutomo
490 Eccles Ave.
South San Francisco, CA 94080-1901
(650) 737-8888
www.yasutomo.com
Papyrus 21 Handmade Papermaking Kit (Starry
Book, p. 69; Heart-Shaped Gift Tag, p. 76)

Paper Adventures
P.O. Box 04393
Milwaukee, WI 53204-0393
(800) 727-0699
www.paperadventures.com
Paper Adventures Violet Petals; Paper Adventures
Opal Flakes (Starry Book, p. 69; Heart-Shaped Gift
Tag, p. 76)

Clipper-Mill
P.O. Box 420376
San Francisco, CA 94142
(415) 552-5005
www.clippermill.com/sponge.html
Pop-up Sponges (Heart-Shaped Gift Tag, p. 76)

mosaic supplies

Diamond Tech
5600-C Airport Blvd.
Tampa, FL 33634
(800) 937-9593
www.jennifersmosaics.com
Vintage Mosaics China Rose Pattern (Mosaic
Trunk, p. 109)

Plaid Enterprises, Inc.
3225 Westech Dr.
Norcross, GA 30092-3500
(800) 842-4197
www.plaidonline.com
Make-It Mosaics tile chips; tile nippers; tile
adhesive; sponge; grout (Mosaic Trunk, p. 109;
China Mosaic Frame, p. 113)

Walnut Hollow Farm, Inc.
1409 State Rd. 23
Dodgeville, WI 35533-2112
(800) 950-5101
www.walnuthollow.com
Square Frame (China Mosaic Frame, p. 113)

Stampington & Company
22992 Mill Creek, Suite B
Laguna Hills, CA 92653
(949) 380-7318
www.stampington.com
Small Papier Mâché Treasure Chest Trunk (Mosaic
Trunk, p. 109)

In the UK:
Edgar Udny & Co Ltd.
314 Balham High
Balham, London
SW17
0181 767 8181

KPTiles: www.kptiles.com
Delphi Glass: www.delphiglass.com
Mosaic Tile Supply:
www.mosaicsupply.com
Mountaintop Mosaics:
www.mountaintopmosaics.com
Mosaic Mercantile: www.mosaicmerc.com

metal & wire supplies

Toner
699 Silver St.
Agawam, MA 01001
(800) 723-1792
www.tonerplastics.com
Fun Wire (plastic-coated) (Tablecloth Weights, p. 83)

American Art Clay Co., Inc. (AMACO)
4717 W. 16th St.
Indianapolis, IN 46222
(800) 374-1600
www.amaco.com
Art Emboss Copper Lightweight Foil Sheet (Aged-Copper Book, p. 86)

C.A.T.S. Group
PO Box 12
Saxmundham
IP17 3NT
+44 (1)728 648717
www.catsgroup.co.uk
ArtEmboss foil

ADDITIONAL ONLINE SUPPLIERS
Metalliferous, Inc.: www.metalliferous.com
Artistic Wire: www.artisticwire.com
Nature's Emporium (tumbled rocks):
natures-emporium.com/
tumbledstones.html

silk floral supplies

Toner
699 Silver St.
Agawam, MA 01001
(800) 723-1792
www.tonerplastics.com
Fun Wire (plastic-coated) (Hydrangea Topiary, p. 95)

ADDITIONAL ONLINE SUPPLIERS
Afloral: www.afloral.com
Silk Greenhouse: www.silkgreenhouse.com
Silk Flowers Express:
www.silkflowersexpress.com

recommended books on creativity

Cameron, Julia. *The Artist's Way: A Spiritual Path to Higher Creativity* (New York: J.P. Tarcher/Putnam, 2002).

Falter-Barns, Suzanne. *How Much Joy Can You Stand?: A Creative Guide to Facing Your Fears and Making Dreams Come True* (New York: Ballentine Wellspring, 2000).
Grout, Pam. *Art and Soul: 156 Ways to Free Your Creative Spirit* (Kansas City, MO: Andrews & McMeel Publishing, 2000).

Louden, Jennifer. *The Comfort Queen's Guide to Life: Create All That You Need with Just What You've Got* (New York: Harmony Books, 2000).

Messer, Mari. *Pencil Dancing: New Ways to Free Your Creative Spirit* (Cincinnati, OH: Walking Stick Press, 2001).

Meekin, Gail. *The 12 Secrets of Highly Creative Women: A Portable Mentor* (Berkeley, CA: Conari Press, 2000).

Sark. *Succulent Wild Woman: Dancing with Your Wonder-Full Self!* (New York: Simon & Schuster, 1997).

Williamson, Marianne. *A Woman's Worth* (New York: Random House, 1993).

recommended magazines

GENERAL CRAFTS

Crafts Magazine
P.O. Box 56015
Boulder, CO 80322
(800) 727-2387
www.craftsmag.com

Expression Magazine
591 Camino de la Reina, Suite 200
San Diego, CA 92108
(619) 819-4520
www.expressionartmagazine.com

Arts & Crafts Magazine
700 E. State St.
Iola, WI 54990
(715) 445-4612
www.artsandcraftsmag.com

Crafting Traditions Magazine
Reiman Publications
5400 S. 60th St.
Greendale, WI 53129
(800) 344-6913
www.craftingtraditions.com

CraftWorks Magazine
All American Crafts, Inc.
243 Newton-Sparta Road
Newton, NJ 07860
(973) 383-8080
www.craftworksmag.com

Crafts 'n Things Magazine
Clapper Communications Companies
2400 Devon, Suite 375
Des Plaines, IL 60018-4618
(800) CRAFTS-1
www.craftideas.com

Quick & Easy Crafts Magazine
House of White Birches
306 E. Park Rd.
Berne, IN 46711
(260) 589-4000
www.quickandeasycrafts.com

Arts & Crafts Canada
P.O. Box 1870
83 Queen Street East,
St. Marys, Ontario
N4X 1C2
(877) 565-2787
www.artsandcraftscanada.com

RUBBER STAMPING

Somerset Studio Magazine
The Stamper's Sampler Magazine
Stampington Inspirations
22992 Mill Creek, Suite B
Laguna Hills, CA 92653
(877) STAMPER
www.somersetstudio.com/html/
  main_magazines.html

RubberStampMadness
P.O. Box 610
Corvallis, OR 97339-0610
(877) STAMPMA
www.rsmadness.com

Craft Stamper UK
Traplet House, Severn Dr.
Upton-upon-Severn
Worcestershire, England
WR8 0JL
+44 (0) 1684 595300
www.craftstamper.com

Stamping Arts and Crafts Magazine
30595 8 Mile Rd.
Livonia, MI 48152
(800) 458-8237
www.scottpublications.com/sacmag

The Rubber Stamper Magazine
P.O. Box 102
Morganville, NJ 07751-0102
(800) 260-9028
www.rubberstamper.com

CRAFT AND DECORATIVE PAINTING

Decorative Artist's Workbook Magazine
4700 E. Galbraith Rd.
Cincinnati, OH 45236
(513) 531-2690 ext. 1461
www.decorativeartist.com

Painting Magazine
Clapper Communications Companies
2400 Devon, Suite 375
Des Plaines, IL 60018-4618
(800) CRAFTS-1
www.paintingmag.com

PaintWorks Magazine
All American Crafts, Inc.
243 Newton-Sparta Rd.
Newton, NJ 07860
(973) 383-8080
www.paintworksmag.com

Tole World Magazine
Wood Strokes & Woodcrafts
1041 Shary Circle
Concord, CA 94518
(925) 671-9852
www.toleworld.com
www.woodstrokes.com

index

Get creative
with North Light Books!

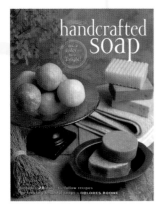

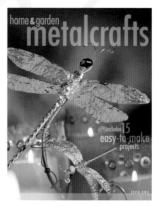

Handcrafted Soap

Create your own luxurious bars of soap today—the kind that lather, clean and smell better than store-bought—and start babying your skin tonight. Simply combine ingredients, cook as directed, add fragrances, place in molds and voilá! Using equipment no more complex than your oven or crock pot, you've made soap that'll be ready to use in an hour!

ISBN 1-58180-268-4, paperback, 128 pages, #32138-K

Home & Garden Metalcrafts

You can create gorgeous home décor and garden art using today's new, craft-friendly metals, meshes and wire. You'll find 15 projects inside, ranging from lamps to picture frames. Most can be completed in an afternoon! You'll learn how to texture, antique and emboss your work, then embellish it with glass beads, scented candles, colorful ribbons and more.

ISBN 1-58180-330-3, paperback, 96 pages, #32296-K

Silk Florals for the Holidays

Make your holidays brighter and more special by creating your very own floral décor! Cele Kahle shows you how to create a variety of gorgeous arrangements, swags, topiaries, wreaths and even bows. There are 19 creative projects in all, using silk foliage, berries, fruit and ribbon. Each one comes with materials lists, step-by-step guidelines and beautiful full-color photos.

ISBN 1-58180-259-5, paperback, 128 pages, #32124-K

30-Minute Rubber Stamp Workshop

Let Sandra McCall show you how to make gorgeous rubber stamp treasures in 30 minutes or less. From home décor and party favors to desk accessories and wearable gifts, you'll find 27 exciting projects inside. Each one is easy to do and inexpensive to make—perfect for those days when you want to create something quick!

ISBN 1-58180-271-4, paperback, 128 pages, #32142-K

These and other fine North Light titles are available from your local art & craft retailer, bookstore, online supplier or by calling 1-800-448-0915.